THE CATHOLIC UNIVERSITY OF AMERICA
CANON LAW STUDIES
No. 193

Judicial Exceptions

CANONICAL COMMENTARY WITH HISTORICAL SYNOPSIS AND HISTORICAL NOTES

A DISSERTATION

Submitted to the Faculty of the School of Canon Law of the Catholic University of America in Partial Fulfillment of the Requirements for the Degree of Doctor of Canon Law

BY
PAUL R. COYLE, A.B., J.C.L.
Priest of the Diocese of Pittsburgh

THE CATHOLIC UNIVERSITY OF AMERICA PRESS
WASHINGTON, D. C.
1944

Nihil Obstat:
LUDOVICUS MOTRY, S.T.D., J.C.D.,
Censor Deputatus.
Washingtonii, D. C., die 23 apr., 1944.

Imprimatur:
✠ HUGO C. BOYLE,
Episcopus Pittsburgensis.
Pittsburghi, die 1 maii, 1944.

Printed by
THE PAULIST PRESS
401 WEST 59TH STREET
NEW YORK 19, N. Y.

 51

TO MY MOTHER

AND TO THE

MEMORY OF

MY FATHER

TABLE OF CONTENTS

CHAPTER V

CHAPTER VI

CHAPTER VII

FOREWORD

The analysis of the institute of the *exceptio* as presented in this dissertation confines itself to the exceptions specifically indicated by name in the Code of Canon Law. Moreover, the study does not seek to exhaust the substantive law on the exceptions presented, but rather to consider the elements of the law which are essential to the application of the principles in procedural practice.

The exception, as understood in Canon Law, differs from the American Civil Law acceptation of the same term. Canon Law employs the term to denote the retarding or eliding of an action of the plaintiff, while the Civil Law uses the same term to indicate an objection raised against a ruling of the court.[1] This dissertation will be concerned only with the canonical aspects of the term. Certain civil statutes will be considered, however, but only insofar as these have been canonized and made part of the substantive law of the single exceptions.

The writer expresses his deepest gratitude to Most Rev. Hugh C. Boyle, Bishop of Pittsburgh, for the opportunity to pursue the course in Canon Law. Sincere sentiments of appreciation are also extended to the members of the Faculty of the School of Canon Law for their kind assistance in the preparation of this work.

1 Bouvier, *Law Dictionary and Concise Encyclopedia* (8. edition, 3. revision by F. Rowle, 3 vols., Kansas City, Mo., 1914), s.v. "Exception."

CHAPTER I

NATURE AND EFFECTS OF EXCEPTIONS

ARTICLE I. GENERAL NOTIONS

AUTHORS distinguish a twofold consideration of the institute of exceptions, viz., first, in a wide sense, by identifying it with every defense which a defendant may use, and secondly, in a strict sense, by limiting its scope to those specific means by which a defendant is legally qualified to retard or elide an action instituted against him.[1] It will be the purpose of this treatise to consider the exception only in the strict sense.

Reiffenstuel (1641-1703) [2] retained the classical definition given by the Roman jurist Ulpian: *Exceptio dicta est quasi quaedam exclusio, quae interponi actioni cujusque rei solet ad excludendum id quod in intentionem, condemnationemve deductum est.*[3] A more accurate description is given by modern authors. They indicate it to be

[1] Pirhing, *Jus Canonicum Nova Methodo Explicatum* (ed. novissima, 2 vols., Dilingae, 1722), lib. II, tit. XXV, n. 1; Schmalzgrueber, *Ius Ecclesiasticum Universum* (5 vols. in 12, Romae, 1843-1845), lib. II, tit. XXV, n. 1; Reiffenstuel, *Ius Canonicum Universum* (5 vols. in 7, Parisiis, 1864-1882), lib. II, tit. XXV, n. 4; Devoti, *Institutionum Canonicarum Libri IV* (4. ed. Romana, Leodii, 1874), lib. II, tit. XXV, n. 1; Lega, *Praelectiones in Textum Iuris Canonici de Iudiciis Ecclesiasticis, De Iudiciis Ecclesiasticis Civilibus* (2. ed., 2 vols., Romae, 1905), I, n. 170; Wernz, *Ius Decretalium* (2. ed., 6 vols., Romae et Prati, 1906-1913), V, n. 410; Noval, *Commentarium Codicis Iuris Canonici, Liber IV, De Processibus, Pars I, De Iudiciis* (Augustae Taurinorum-Romae, 1920), n. 297; Roberti, *De Processibus* (2 vols., Romae: apud Aedes Facultatis Iuridicae ad S. Apollinaris, 1926), n. 272; De Meester, *Juris Canonici et Juris Canonico-Civilis Compendium* (ed. nova, 3 vols. in 4, Brugis: Desclée de Brouwer, 1921-1928), n. 1561. Hereafter, the works of Pirhing, Schmalzgrueber, Reiffenstuel, and Devoti indicated above will be cited by the authors' names.

[2] Lib. II, tit. XXV, n. 2.

[3] D (44.1) 2.

an assertion of the defendant against a fact or right of the plaintiff by which the latter's action is delayed or estopped.[4]

Exceptions in the strict sense truly suppose that the plaintiff has a valid action, but due to some circumstance independent of the basis of the claim the action is liable to delay or complete nullification by virtue of an exception registered by the defendant.[5] For example, a plaintiff's action may be delayed because the judge in his case is incompetent or suspect, rather than because his complaint is without foundation in fact. Likewise, a plaintiff may have a *prima facie* claim of ownership of an object, but if the defendant presents and succeeds in proving the exception of prescription the suit will be quashed.

The defendant, in employing the exception in his plan of defense, takes on the aspect of being a plaintiff, for through the exception he questions the accuser's status in the particular case. By this fact, he takes upon himself the burden of proving the exception.[6] An exception differs from an action, however, inasmuch as the plaintiff attempts to establish his right in court by means of his action, whereas a defendant, with the exception, attempts to exclude the action.[7]

An exception is distinguished from a replication, since the latter is used by the plaintiff as a rebuttal to the exception, questioning

[4] Wernz, *Ius Decretalium,* V, 410; Lega, *De Iudiciis Ecclesiasticis,* I, p. 170; Noval, *De Iudiciis,* n. 293; Roberti, *De Processibus,* n. 272; De Meester, *Compendium,* n. 1561; Coronata, *Institutiones Iuris Canonici* (5 vols., Taurini: Marietti, Vols. I-II, 2. ed., 1939; Vols. III-IV-V, 1933-1935-1936), III, n. 1194; Król, *The Defendant in Contentious Trials,* The Catholic University of America Canon Law Studies, n. 146 (Washington, D. C.: The Catholic University of America Press, 1942), p. 103.

[5] Roberti, *De Processibus,* n. 272; Coronata, *Institutiones,* n. 1194.

[6] Roberti, *De Processibus,* n. 272; Noval, *De Iudiciis,* n. 300.

[7] Schmalzgrueber, lib. II, tit. XXV, n. 1; Bouix, *Tractatus de Iudiciis Ecclesiasticis* (2 vols., Parisiis, 1855), II, 169, 176 (hereafter cited *De Iudiciis Ecclesiasticis*); Smith, *Elements of Ecclesiastical Law* (5. ed., 3 vols., New York, 1883-1887), II, 200, 212; Lega, *De Iudiciis Ecclesiasticis,* I, 170; Noval, *De Iudiciis,* n. 298.

the right of the defendant to place the exception.[8] This has the effect of eliding the exception.[9]

Formerly, Cardinal Hostiensis (+1271)[10] identified the term replication with the term exception. This connotation multiplies the aspects of an exception, since the defendant, upon hearing the replication, could place what is called a *duplicatio,* and then the plaintiff a *triplicatio,* the defendant a *quadruplicatio,* etc. According to this sense each of these may be called an exception. It is the duty of the judge, however, to limit an endless contest of this kind and to insure the defendant the right to the final plea.[11]

Exceptions may be both *personal* and *real* in nature. Those which may be claimed only by a certain defendant on account of particular circumstances which limit the use of the exception to that defendant are termed personal, *scil.,* those which are not incumbent upon heirs and sureties of the defendant. Real exceptions concern the nature of the case or a matter which does not depend upon the identity of the defendant for their efficacy.[12] All exceptions are held to be real until it is clear from the law or contract that they are personal.[13]

Also with regard to their nature, exceptions may be *substantial* or *processual,* according as they concern the merits of the case or the form of procedure respectively.[14]

As to their effect, exceptions may be *peremptory* or *dilatory.* Peremptory exceptions obstruct the action of the plaintiff perpetually, or completely destroy his right to sue in the particular case. Those

[8] C. 2, X, *de exceptionibus,* II, 25; Pirhing, lib. II, tit. XXV, n. 2; Barbosa, *Collectanea Doctorum, tam Veterum quam Recentiorum in Jus Pontificium Universum* (5 vols., Lugduni, 1637), c. 2, lib. II, tit. XXV, nn. 1-3 (hereafter cited by name of author); Devoti, lib. II, tit. XXV, n. 10; Roberti, *De Processibus,* n. 272; Noval, *De Iudiciis,* n. 299.

[9] Wernz, *Ius Decretalium,* V, n. 425; Noval, *De Iudiciis,* n. 299.

[10] Henricus Cardinalis Hostiensis, *Summa Aurea, tit. De Exceptionibus,* § *Quid sit* (ed. Venetiis, 1570), f. 180v.

[11] Noval, *De Iudiciis,* n. 299.

[12] Pirhing, lib. II, tit. XXV, n. 2; Devoti, lib. II, tit. XXV, n. 1; Wernz, *Ius Decretalium,* V, n. 411; Bouix, *De Iudiciis Ecclesiasticis,* II, 170; Roberti, *De Processibus,* n. 273.

[13] Wernz, *Ius Decretalium,* V, n. 411, note 9.

[14] Roberti, *De Processibus,* n. 273.

which bar action and wipe out the suit completely are named *peremptoriae litis finitae*. Those which merely destroy the right to sue but allow the possibility of the consideration of the case on its own merits are called simple peremptory exceptions.[15] The basis of the peremptory exception constitutes an intimate part of the object of the suit and may even be identified with it. Otherwise it would not have the definitive effect it has on the decision of the cause. For example, when a peremptory exception of the *litis finitae* category (i. e. an exception based on the fact that the matter has already been decided) is proposed, the introduction of the action will be barred and the one proposing the exception will have vindicated his right. In like manner, one who places and proves a simple peremptory exception will gain a favorable decision in the definitive sentence because such an exception is associated with the merits of the cause so intimately that a decision on the validity of such an exception will necessarily affect the definitive sentence. For example, if a plaintiff seeks the execution of a contract, a defendant who was induced by grave fear *ab extrinseco* to enter into the contract may register an exception accordingly and thus gain a favorable decision.

Dilatory exceptions are those which postpone the placing of an action for a time, or delay the issue temporarily.[16] Those which postpone the placing of an action for a time are called *dilatoriae solutionis;* those which merely delay the trial are called *dilatoriae iudicii.*[17] For example, an action may not be placed until the cause

[15] Pirhing, lib. II, tit. XXV, n. 2; Schmalzgrueber, lib. II, tit. XXV, n. 4; Reiffenstuel, lib. II, tit. XXV, n. 13; Devoti, lib. II, tit. XXV, n. 6; Bouix, *De Iudiciis Ecclesiasticis,* II, 170; Smith, *Elements of Ecclesiastical Law,* II, 197; Wernz, *Ius Decretalium,* V, n. 411; Roberti, *De Processibus,* n. 273; Noval. *De Iudiciis,* n. 299; Coronata, *Institutiones,* n. 1195; De Meester, *Compendium,* n. 1550; Vermeersch-Creusen, *Epitome Iuris Canonici* (3 vols., Mechliniae-Romae: H. Dessain, 1931), III, n. 68 (hereafter cited *Epitome*).

[16] Pirhing, lib. II, tit. XXV, n. 2; Schmalzgrueber, lib. II, tit. XXV, n. 5; Reiffenstuel, lib. II, tit. XXV, n. 13; Devoti, lib. II, tit. XXV, n. 2; Bouix, *De Iudiciis Ecclesiasticis,* II, 171; Smith, *Elements of Ecclesiastical Law,* II, 197; Wernz, *Ius Decretalium,* V, n. 411; Roberti, *loc. cit.*; Noval, *loc. cit.*; Coronata, *loc. cit.*; De Meester, *loc. cit.*; Vermeersch-Creusen, *loc. cit.*

[17] Gloss, to *Dict. Grat.* p.c. 2, C. III, q. 6. Later authors do not retain this distinction found in the gloss of the *Decretum Gratiani.* However, it is a plausible one since it describes more accurately the exact nature of the exception.

of the action has matured. If a plaintiff should seek the payment of a debt which will not be due until some future date, an exception indicating that payment is not yet due may be raised, thus postponing the action until the defendant is truly delinquent. Also, the trial in which a legitimate action has been introduced may be postponed, e.g. until the case is referred to the competent forum, until a judge is substituted for one who is suspect, until an excommunicated person has obtained absolution from his censure, etc.

Article II. Peremptory Exceptions

Among the exceptions which are introduced to show that the action of the plaintiff is both set aside and barred are the *res iudicata,* previous compromise, decisory oath, previous arbitration, payment, and a contract not to enter suit.[18] These are the *litis finitae* exceptions. When exceptions of this type are proved the judge will rule that the cause has already been decided and hence that the one against whom the exception is placed may not prosecute the cause further. The *res iudicata* would be based on a previous court decision; the compromise or arbitration would be based on contracts which will eliminate the possibility of prosecuting the cause; the decisory oath would decide the issue when the party is challenged to take such an oath and proof of its existence would bar suit; payment of a debt would necessarily eliminate prosecution on the basis of non-payment; a contract not to enter suit would be effective in setting aside such a suit. Each of these exceptions will be considered in detail in a later chapter.

Among the exceptions which may wipe out the action and are judged according to the merits of the case are prescription, fraud, fear and error.[19] These exceptions do not decide the issue so definitely as those of the *litis finitae* category. They will be considered accordingly as they affect the object of the suit. They will be effec-

[18] Schmalzgrueber, lib. II, tit. XXV, n. 4; Bouix, *De Iudiciis Ecclesiasticis,* II, 170; Smith, *Elements of Ecclesiastical Law,* II, p. 197; Roberti, *De Processibus,* n. 175; Noval, *De Iudiciis,* n. 299; Coronata, *Institutiones,* III, n. 1195.

[19] Schmalzgrueber, lib. II, tit. XXV, n. 4; Bouix, *De Iudiciis Ecclesiasticis,* II, 170; Roberti, *De Processibus,* n. 175; Noval, *De Iudiciis,* n. 299.

tive in determining the final decision according to the degree of their effect on the principal cause. Ownership may be transferred by prescription and acts may be rescinded when performed under the influence of grave fear or as a result of fraud, hence the determining effect of these exceptions. Each of these will be considered in detail in a later chapter.

ARTICLE III. DILATORY EXCEPTIONS

Dilatory exceptions which fall into the category *dilatoriae solutionis* concern those cases in which the right of action has not yet matured. For example, the plaintiff does not have the right to sue until the date set for payment of a debt has passed. Nor may he propose suit if he has made an agreement that he will not sue for a definite period. Suit will not be permitted until the time agreed upon has elapsed.[20] The defendant may register an exception accordingly.

More common are the exceptions which are *dilatoriae iudicii.* These concern suits which may be postponed because there is some defect in the legal procedure. They may be alleged against the persons of the judge, the auditor, assessor, the promoter of justice, the defender of the bond, the plaintiff and his procurator, the time or the place of the trial, a defective libellus, and spoliation.[21]

Exceptions which are proposed against the person of the judge may indicate that he is incompetent, suspect or ignorant of the law.[22] These are given the special title *declinatoriae fori* because they are

[20] Gloss to *Dict. Grat.* p.c. 2, C. III, q. 6.

[21] Pirhing, lib. II, tit. XXV, n. 2; Schmalzgrueber, lib. II, tit. XXV, n. 5; Reiffenstuel, lib. II, tit. XXV, nn. 13, 14; Bouix, *De Iudiciis Ecclesiasticis,* II, 171; Smith, *Elements of Ecclesiastical Law,* II, 197, 198; Wernz, *Ius Decretalium,* V, n. 411; Roberti, *De Processibus,* n. 175; Noval, *De Iudiciis,* n. 299.

[22] Canons 1613; 1614; Schmalzgrueber, lib. II, tit. XXV, n. 4; Reiffenstuel, lib. II, tit. XXV, n. 13; Pirhing, lib. II, tit. XXV, n. 2; Bouix, *De Iudiciis Ecclesiasticis,* II, 171, 179; *Smith, Elements of Ecclesiastical Law,* II, 202; Wernz, *Ius Decretalium,* V, n. 411; S.R.R., *Decisiones, coram R.P.D. Lega,* 11 maii, 1909, decis. V, n. 4—*Decisiones,* I (1912), 39; *coram R.P.D., Lega,* 31 maii, 1912, decis. XXIII, n. 10—*Decisiones,* IV (1917), 279.

opposed to or tend to decline the particular tribunal.[23] The exception of suspicion may be placed against the promoter of justice, defender of the bond and other members of the tribunal.[24] The exception of incompetency is based on the fact that the cause in question does not come within the jurisdiction of the court against which the exception is raised. The exception of suspicion is based on a relationship that exists or formerly existed between the parties in the cause and the personnel of the court.

A plaintiff or his procurator may be excluded for the reason that they are excommunicated.[25] An exception may also be placed against the procurator if he does not have a proper mandate from the person he represents.[26]

An exception may be placed against the time fixed for the trial, that it does not provide sufficient opportunity to amass the necessary proofs.[27] Another may indicate that the place of the trial does not insure a safe or just procedure, or that it is too far distant.[28]

An exception may be placed against the libellus due to the fact that it does not contain mention of the cause of action [29] or because it is otherwise defective.[30]

A defendant may claim the *exceptio spolii* if he has been despoiled of his goods by the plaintiff. He is not bound to reply to the charges of his adversary until full restitution has been made.[31]

[23] Noval, *De Iudiciis*, n. 299.

[24] Canon 1614, § 3.

[25] Canons 1654; 2263; 2256; 1657; Pirhing, lib. II, tit. XXV, n. 2; Schmalzgrueber, lib. II, tit. XXV, n. 5; Bouix, *De Iudiciis Ecclesiasticis*, II, 170; Wernz, *Ius Decretalium*, V, n. 411; Noval, *De Iudiciis*, n. 299; Roberti, *De Processibus*, n. 175.

[26] Canon 1659, § 1; c. 4, X, *de procuratoribus*, I, 38; Schmalzgrueber, lib. II, tit. XXV, n. 5; Bouix, *De Iudiciis Ecclesiasticis*, II, 170; Wernz, *Ius Decretalium*, V, n. 411; Noval, *De Iudiciis*, n. 299; Roberti, *De Processibus*, n. 175.

[27] Noval, *De Iudiciis*, n. 299.

[28] Noval, *loc. cit.*

[29] Pirhing, lib. II, tit. XXV, n. 2; Schmalzgrueber, lib. II, tit. XXV, n. 5; Reiffenstuel, lib. II, tit. XXV, n. 14; Bouix, *De Iudiciis Ecclesiasticis*, II, 181; Wernz, *Ius Decretalium*, V, n. 411.

[30] Roberti, *De Processibus*, n. 175.

[31] Canons 1670, §§ 1, 2; 1699, § 1; c. 1. C. III, q. 1; c. 2, X, *de ordine cognitionum*, II, 10; c. 4, X, *de ordine cognitionum*, II, 10; Schmalzgrueber,

Article IV. Duration of Exceptions

While actions are temporal in nature and may be circumscribed by time limits as to their presentation in court, exceptions are perpetual and are not usually affected by any temporal limitations.[32] The reason for this difference consists in the fact that a plaintiff is free to propose suit and may do so within a convenient time, while the defendant is not free but depends upon the will of his opponent.[33] The defendant thus has the right to protect himself against an unjust aggressor who could otherwise easily use the time element to his own advantage.[34]

Some exceptions, however, may cease by tacit renunciation,[35] or by the legal specification which requires that they be placed at a certain time, v.g., before the joinder of issue.[36] In both these instances the time element does not begin to run until the process is under way, thus leaving the perpetual nature of the exception undisturbed substantially.

An exception, therefore, is always available as long as the facts upon which the exception is based exist and as long as the legal requirements for its presentation in court are observed.

Article V. The Legal Use of Exceptions

The right to place an exception is readily admitted.[37] The origin of this right, however, has been disputed among the authors. Some have claimed that its origin is in the natural law inasmuch as it is

lib. II, tit. XXV, n. 5; Reiffenstuel, lib. II, tit. XXV, n. 13; Smith, *Elements of Ecclesiastical Law*, II, 198; Wernz, *Ius Decretalium*, V, n. 508; Noval, *De Iudiciis*, n. 365; De Meester, *Compendium*, n. 1571; Coronata, *Institutiones*, n. 1202.

32 Canon 1667.

33 Roberti, *De Processibus*, n. 275.

34 Noval, *De Iudiciis*, n. 301.

35 Noval, *loc. cit.*

36 Canon 1628.

37 "Qui ad agendum admittitur, est ad excipiendum multo magis admittendus," Reg. 71, R.J. in VI°; S. C. Ep. et Reg., *Lublinen.*, 8 mart. 1898—*Fontes*, n. 2034.

a means of defense based on that law.[38] Others have maintained that it was introduced by the positive law just as an action is an invention of the positive law. They conclude this because an exception consists in the exclusion of an action. These also claim that the right to use an exception may be taken away by an act of the legislator, which would not be the case if exceptions were based on the natural law.[39] Gonzalez-Tellez (+ ca. 1674) [40] identified with the natural law only those exceptions which were introduced for a just and necessary defense. He maintained that those which were not necessary to the defense could be regulated by the human legislator. This seems to be the opinion generally accepted today.[41]

Exceptions may be placed by defendants, by their heirs, and the sureties of both, unless they are personal.[42] The use of personal exceptions do not pass on to anyone else. Nor do the *exceptiones reales* pass from one surety to another.[43] But the *exceptiones reales* may be used by the surety of the defendant, even if the defendant is unwilling to co-operate.[44]

Schmalzgrueber (1663-1735) [45] proposed the doubt whether an excommunicated person would or would not be allowed the use of exceptions. He adhered to the affirmative opinion.[46] Although an excommunicated person may be rejected as a plaintiff,[47] he is con-

[38] Schmalzgrueber, lib. II, tit. XXV, n. 7; Bouix, *De Iudiciis Ecclesiasticis*, II, 169; Wernz, *Ius Decretalium*, V, n. 413; Coronata, *Institutiones*, III, n. 1201.

[39] Schmalzgrueber, lib. II, tit. XXV, n. 7.

[40] *Commentaria Perpetua in singulos textus quinque librorum Decretalium Gregorii IX* (5 vols., Venetiis, 1699), lib. II, tit. XXV, n. 6.

[41] Noval, *De Iudiciis*, n. 298.

[42] Pirhing, lib. II, tit. XXV, n. 4; Zoesius, lib. II, tit. XXV, n. 4; Reiffenstuel, lib. II, tit. XXV, n. 79; Wernz, *Ius Decretalium*, V, n. 413.

[43] Hostiensis, *Summa Aurea*, f. 182v.

[44] Ricardus Anglicus, *Die Summa de Ordine Iudiciario* (ed. Wahrmund, *Quellen zur Geschicte des römisch-kanonischen Processes in Mittelalter*, II, 3 (5 vols., Innsbruck, 1905-1928), 98; Reiffenstuel, lib. II, tit. XXV, n. 79.

[45] Lib. II, tit. XXV, n. 12.

[46] *Loc. cit.*

[47] Canon 1628, § 3; C. 20, X, *de accusationibus, inquisitionibus, et de denuntiationibus*, V, 1.

sidered to be permitted the use of exceptions in order to secure an equitable defense.[48]

Since it is the function of the defender of the bond to defend the validity of marriages,[49] it will be his duty to interpose any exceptions which may tend to delay the trial, quash or bar the suit. His activities in this regard will follow the procedure of the ordinary defendant in contentious cases.

Likewise, the promoter of justice as a public official seeking to secure the rights of the Church when the common good is concerned [50] has the right to propose exceptions in the interest of justice.

The judge is not to advert to any exception *ex officio* except the fact of excommunication against one who is a *vitandus* or one against whom a declaratory or condemnatory sentence has been pronounced.[51]

Ordinarily, if the defendant does not produce the exceptions which are available to him, the judge is not to supply them.[52] In purely private causes the defendant must indicate the exception, otherwise he is considered to have renounced his right.[53] If, however, the public good or the salvation of souls is concerned in the cause, the judge can and ought to supply them.[54]

In criminal causes, matrimonial causes, causes concerning sacred ordination [55] and causes wherein moral persons are concerned [56] the

[48] Schmalzgrueber, lib. II, tit. XXV, n. 12; Wernz, *Ius Decretalium*, V, n. 413; Noval, *De Iudiciis*, n. 299.

[49] Canon 1568; Dolan, *The Defensor Vinculi, His Rights and Duties*, The Catholic University of America Canon Law Studies, n. 85 (Washington, D. C.: The Catholic University of America, 1934), p. xi; Wernz-Vidal, *Ius Canonicum*, VI, n. 111; Benedictus XIV, const. *"Dei Miseratione,"* n. 6—*Fontes*, n. 318.

[50] Vermeersch-Creusen, *Epitome*, III, n. 43; Coronata, *Institutiones*, n. 1124; Noval, *De Iudiciis*, n. 140; Glynn, *The Promoter of Justice*, The Catholic University of America Canon Law Studies, n. 101 (Washington, D. C.: The Catholic University of America, 1936), xix.

[51] Canon 1628, § 3.

[52] Canon 1619, § 1.

[53] Wernz, *Ius Decretalium*, V, n. 418; Noval, *De Iudiciis*, n. 204; De Meester, *Compendium*, n. 1547.

[54] Canon 1619, § 2.

[55] Roberti, *De Processibus*, n. 169.

[56] Canons 103, § 3; 1688, § 2.

judge must question the parties on matters involving the common good.[57] Hence any exceptions which are brought forth in this investigation will be adverted to directly.

These general rules for proofs are applied to *substantial* exceptions as well.[58] Also, on account of the public nature of the process, several *processual* exceptions are likewise to be revealed by the judge *ex officio*, viz., competence,[59] suspicion,[60] capacity of the parties, the mandate of the procurator, a pending trial,[61] nullity of sentence [62] and the *res iudicata*.[63]

There is no objection to placing several exceptions at the same time.[64] This is true since exceptions are legitimate means of defense, a plurality of which is not prohibited.[65]

The advantage of placing several exceptions at the same time consists in the fact that if the defendant is unable to prove one he may pass on to the proof of another.[66] The several exceptions made by the defendant may even be contradictory in the facts they allege.[67] The only requirement is that they be proposed alternatively with the intention that, if the proof of one should be deficient, recourse may be had to another.[68] For example, the defendant may make the contrary claims to the effect that a debt which he is being called upon to pay has been paid, or, if not paid, that it never really

[57] Canon 1742, § 1.

[58] Roberti, *De Processibus*, n. 169.

[59] Canons 1609, § 1; 1611.

[60] Canon 1613, § 1.

[61] Roberti, *De Processibus*, n. 169.

[62] Canon 1897, § 2.

[63] Roberti, *De Processibus*, n. 169.

[64] Canon 1669, § 2; Pirhing, lib. II, tit. XXV, n. 48; Zoesius, lib. II, tit. XXV, n. 8; Reiffenstuel, lib. II, tit. XXV, n. 96; Bouix, *De Iudiciis Ecclesiasticis*, II, 176; Lega, *De Iudiciis Ecclesiasticis*, I, p. 171; Noval, *De Iudiciis*, n. 306.

[65] "Nullus pluribus uti defensionibus prohibetur"—Reg. 20, R. J. in VI°.

[66] Schmalzgrueber, lib. II, tit. XXV, n. 30.

[67] Canon 1669, § 2.

[68] Noval, *De Iudiciis*, n. 306; Król, *The Defendant in Contentious Trials*, p 105.

existed.[69] This is true since the defendant is not presumed to make confession of the facts contained in the exceptions when they are proposed.[70]

However, if the defendant should expressly admit the existence of his obligation in proposing the exception, he will be held liable to the obligation if the exception is not proved.[71] Coronata [72] warns that the defendant should proceed cautiously lest he should harm himself partially or totally by openly confessing the intention of his opponent by, for example, making the exception in this fashion: "I confess that I owed you $100 as the result of a loan, but I say that I have already paid the $100." Failure to prove the exception will result in his being held for the debt.

The situation, on the other hand, may warrant the exception being placed in the following manner: "I deny that I owed you $100 as the result of a loan, but if the debt did exist, I maintain that it is already paid." [73] In the first case the exception was proposed copulatively, asserting the fact of the debt to be true. In the second case the exceptions were indicated disjunctively or alternatively with no express admission of the intention of the plaintiff.

The objection raised against placing several contrary exceptions at the same time is that the defendant in making use of an exception takes on the aspect of being a plaintiff, and since the plaintiff is denied the use of several conflicting actions at the same time,[74] some have been of the opinion that the defendant should be limited in like manner with regard to the placing of exceptions. Despite this fact, however, the position of the defendant is not really equal

[69] Schmalzgrueber, lib. II, tit. XXV, n. 31; Pirhing, lib. II, tit. XXV, n. 45; Reiffenstuel, lib. II, tit. XXV, nn. 98, 99; Bouix, *De Iudiciis Ecclesiasticis,* II, 176.

[70] C. 6, X, *de exceptionibus,* II, 25; "Exceptionem obiiciens non videtur de intentione adversarii confiteri"—Reg. 63, R.J., in VI°.

[71] Coronata, *Institutiones,* n. 1201.

[72] *Loc. cit.*

[73] Reiffenstuel, lib. II, tit. XXV, n. 25, 90-99; Wernz-Vidal, *Ius Canonicum* (7 tomes in 8 vols., Romae: Apud Aedes Universitatis Gregorianae, Vol. VI, *De Processibus,* 1927), VI, 261.

[74] Canon 1669, § 1.

to that of the plaintiff, for the former is brought into court quite unwillingly and far less prepared.[75]

The exceptions may be placed in any manner, orally or in writing, as long as the right and reason for placing them are clearly indicated and registered in the acts.[76]

[75] Schmalzgrueber, lib. II, tit. XXV, n. 30; Bouix, *De Iudiciis Ecclesiasticis,* II, 176.

[76] Schmalzgrueber, lib. II, tit. XXV, n. 29; Bouix, *De Iudiciis Ecclesiasticis,* II, 176; Wernz, *Ius Decretalium,* V, n. 418; Doheny, *Canonical Procedure in Matrimonial Cases* (Milwaukee: Bruce, 1938), p. 73.

CHAPTER II

HISTORICAL SYNOPSIS

ARTICLE I. ROMAN LAW

THE term *exceptio* had its origin in the processual system of Roman Law according to formulas. In this system the distinction between the law and the judgment of the cause was maintained, i.e., between the presentation of the cause before the pretor or magistrate, and the investigation and decision of the same cause before the judge. The pretor, as the interpreter of the law, decided the question of law involved in the cause, but the judge resolved the question of fact. After the cause was presented to the pretor and the question of law was decided by him, he passed on to the judge the formula or sentence according to which the defendant was to be condemned. If in the presentation of the cause before the pretor the defendant had adduced some reasons of fact which were considered sufficient to delay, bar or quash the action of the plaintiff, the pretor indicated these facts in the formula, prefacing them by the word *exceptio* or *excepto casu.* For example, if Titius registered a claim against Cajus in order to recover a piece of property, the litigants appeared before the pretor, and after Titius had established his intention, the circumstances of the case could warrant that Cajus place the exception to the effect that although it was true that Titius did have the original ownership, that ownership was transferred by prescription. In passing the formula on to the judge, the pretor, after pointing out the law in the matter, could insert the phrase, *excepto casu praescriptionis.*[1]

Hence, the condemnation of the defendant would have been considered the general rule, while the exception to the rule was embodied in the legal use of the *exceptio.* And while in its first significance the exception consisted in the exclusion from the general

[1] Noval, *De Iudiciis,* n. 296.

condemnatory formula, it afterwards came to be synonymous with the facts or allegations upon which the exception was based.[2]

The following peremptory exceptions were recognized in Roman Law and could bar the action of the plaintiff: (a) the *res iudicata,* which was an exception whereby a defendant pleading previous judgment was able not merely to frustrate the repetition of the same action, but also—and this is what is called the positive function of the *exceptio rei iudicatae*—to rebut any subsequent claim directly conflicting with the decision contained in such judgment; [3] (b) the *exceptio pacti conventi perpetui,* which consisted either of an agreement not to enter suit, or of a settlement out of court; [4] (c) the *exceptio praescriptionis,* by virtue of which the tenure of property for thirty years could bar suit.[5]

Among the simple peremptory exceptions, which allowed the presentation of the cause but could be effective in quashing the suit, were the *exceptio doli mali* and the *exceptio quod metus causa.* The *exceptio doli mali* was a special defense allowed the defendant or his legal successor because of fraud in the act on which the suit was founded.[6] The *exceptio quod metus causa* was a special defense allowed a person who was sued on an act he had performed under the influence of fear.[7]

Among the exceptions which were dilatory with regard to their solution was the *pactum de non petendo,* limited to a certain length of time, which consisted of an agreement not to require the payment of a debt or the solution of an obligation until a certain period had elapsed. This was also termed the *exceptio pacti temporalis.*[8] Among those which were dilatory with regard to the postponing of the trial were those placed against the person of the judge, against the person of the plaintiff and on account of the person of the

[2] Noval, *loc. cit.*

[3] D. (44.1); D. (43.1) 56; Sohm, *The Institutes* (Oxford: Clarendon Press, 1926), p. 286.

[4] Inst. (4.13) 1; Sohm, *op. cit.,* p. 275.

[5] C. (7.39) 9.

[6] D. (44.1) 3.

[7] Sohm, *op. cit.,* p. 209.

[8] D. (44.1) 3; Inst. (4.13) 8.

defendant.[9] The trial would be delayed until another judge was supplied, until the defect in the procedural capacity of the plaintiff was healed, or until the defendant, for example, a legate who had the *ius revocandi domum*,[10] would be cited in the proper court.

Another group of exceptions was called *anomalous* by the authors because they did not follow the general rule of peremptory and dilatory exceptions with regard to the time at which they could be proposed.[11] These were the *exceptio senatusconsulti Macedoniani* and the *exceptio senatusconsulti Velleiani*. The *senatusconsultum Macedonianum* forbade loans of money to a *filiusfamilias*. If a *filiusfamilias* was sued on a loan, the pretor allowed him to plead the *exceptio senatusconsulti Macedoniani*.[12] The *senatusconsultum Velleianum* prohibited women not only from becoming sureties, but from entering into any form of *intercessio*, thus debarring them, for example, from creating a mortgage or accepting a loan in the interest of a third person. A woman who was sued in respect of an *intercessio* of any kind—whether suretyship or any other—could claim the *exceptio senatusconsulti Velleiani*.[13]

With regard to the time for placing exceptions, dilatory exceptions were to be placed in the beginning of the trial, before the joinder of issue.[14] If an advocate placed an omitted dilatory exception after the joinder of issue, a fine of one pound of gold was to be imposed as a penalty.[15] Peremptory exceptions could be placed at any time during the trial.[16] A soldier who had omitted an exception could

[9] Costa, *Profilo Storico del Processo Civile Romano* (Roma, 1918), 161-163; Wenger, *Institutes of the Roman Law of Civil Procedure* (rev. ed., translated by Fisk, New York: Veritas Press, 1940), pp. 284-291.

[10] A legate was not bound to appear in the court of the province to which he was sent, but had the *ius revocandi domum*, or the right to return for a defense to his own province—D. (5.1) (2.3).

[11] Gloss to *Dict. Grat.* p.c. 2, C. III, q. 6; Hostiensis, *Summa Aurea*, f180v; Durantis, *Speculum Iudiciale* (Venetiis, 1577), II, 509.

[12] D. (12.6) 40.

[13] Sohm, *The Institutes*, pp. 277, 386.

[14] C. (4.19) 19.

[15] C. (8.35) 12.

[16] C. (7.33) 9.

introduce it after the sentence.[17] The Macedonian and Velleianian exceptions could also be placed after the sentence.[18]

No one was prohibited the use of several exceptions.[19] Even though these exceptions were different, they were to be admitted.[20]

Article II. Decree of Gratian

The most prominent indication of the law on judicial exceptions in the Decree of Gratian is found in a Pseudo-Isidorian decretal attributed to Pope Fabian (236-250) and declaring that if a bishop was accused of a crime he was to be tried by all the bishops of the province and in the defendant's own court.[21] This decretal was received into the *Decretum Gratiani,* to which Gratian appended the pertinent *dictum* about exceptions that the *exceptio fori* was dilatory and therefore was to be placed and proved in the beginning of the trial.[22]

The gloss to the *dictum* explains the law on exceptions in further detail, pointing out that there are three types of exceptions: dilatory, peremptory and mixed; that dilatory exceptions may be declinatory of judgment and declinatory of solution; that the *exceptio declinatoria iudicii,* which delays the trial itself, must be placed and proved in the beginning of the trial; that the *exceptio dilatoria solutionis,* which delays the placing of an action, was to be placed in the beginning of the trial, but that it was not necessary to prove this exception until after the plaintiff had established his ground of action.

The gloss goes further to show that peremptory exceptions could be placed and proved at any time before the final sentence; that mixed exceptions were so called because they partook of the nature of both dilatory and peremptory exceptions; that they were like dilatory exceptions inasmuch as they could be placed before the

[17] C. (1.18) 1.

[18] D. (14.6) 11.

[19] D. (44.1) 8.

[20] D. (44.1) 8.

[21] C. 2, C. III, q. 6; Hinschius, *Decretales Pseudo-Isidorianae, et Capitula Angilramni* . . . (Lipsiae, 1863), c. 26, p. 167 (hereafter cited *Decretales Pseudo-Isidorianae*).

[22] *Dict. Grat.* p.c. 2, C. III, q. 6.

joinder of issue, and like peremptory exceptions, since they could also be placed after the joinder of issue but before the final sentence. Other exceptions are indicated as anomalous in the same gloss, namely, those which could be placed after the final sentence, such as the *exceptiones SC. Velleiani* and *SC. Macedoniani.*[23]

The *exceptio spolii* as applied to bishops was incorporated into the *Decretum Gratiani* from a Pseudo-Isidorian decretal attributed to Pope Innocent I (401-417).[24] This decretal pointed out that before any crime was to be alleged against any bishop it was necessary to restore to him any goods of which he might have been despoiled, or if he had been deprived of his See that it was to be returned to him before any action could be taken against him.

Article III. Decretal Law

Alexander III (1159-1181) in a mandate given to the Archbishop of York declared that the courts were to admit reasonable exceptions and proceed according to the equity of the law, unless it should be declared by papal pronouncement that no exceptions were to be admitted. At the same time he pointed out that no such limitation of the use of exceptions had been declared by the Holy See, at that time or previously.[25]

The exception of suspicion was officially recognized when Pope Lucius III (1181-1185) decreed that a judge who was related to the plaintiff, or who was his business associate, or who was in any way suspect, could be refused by the defendant. At the same time the Pope pointed out that the cause of the suspicion was to be proposed before the judge against whom the exception was raised, and that it was to be proved before arbiters.[26]

[23] Gloss to *Dict. Grat.* p.c. 2, C. III, q. 6.

[24] C. 1, C. III, q. 1; Hinschius, *Decretales Pseudo-Isidorianae,* 215; Jaffé, *Regesta Pontificum Romanorum ab condita Ecclesia ad annum post Christum natum MCXCVIII* (ed. 2. curaverunt S. Löwenfeld, F. Kaltenbrunner, P. Ewald, 2 vols. in 1, Lipsiae, 1885-1888), (hereafter cited JL, JK, JE), 318.

[25] C. 13, X, *de officio iudicis delegati,* I, 13; *Comp. I,* I, 21, 18; JL, n. 13877.

[26] C. 36, X, *de appellationibus,* II, 28; *Comp. I,* II, 20, 45; JL, n. 14966.

Celestine III (1191-1198) reiterated (June 17, 1193) the law with regard to the exception of suspicion when he indicated that persons who were suspect or who were enemies to those involved in the trial were not to be judges in the case.[27]

The same Pope also declared that if an exception were claimed against a witness alleging that he was guilty of some crime, the witness was not to be allowed to testify. However, such a witness was not to be punished for the crime unless it concerned the point at issue.[28]

The most prolific papal legislator on the law of judicial exceptions was Pope Innocent III (1198-1216). On March 3, 1198, he pointed out that a person who had several benefices was not permitted to make an exception based on a plurality of benefices against someone else.[29]

A very decisive piece of legislation was issued by this Pope on December 19, 1204, when he decreed that a definite time limit was to be assigned by the judge after the expiration of which limit exceptions were not to be admitted. He indicated certain exemptions from this law which would allow some dilatory exceptions to be admitted after the time limit. These exemptions were based on three main contingencies: (1) that the defendant should apply before the time limit for permission to make a particular exception later; (2) that something new should arise after the time limit which did not exist before; (3) that an exception which existed before should come to the knowledge of the defendant only after the time limit. This latter fact was to be sealed by the defendant's oath.[30]

On February 1, 1207, Innocent III declared that the *exceptio falsi procuratoris* could be placed not only before but also after the sentence of the judge. Thus the sentence could be rendered null and

[27] C. 41, X, *de appellationibus*, II, 28; *Comp. II*, II, 19, 16; JL, n. 17019.

[28] C. I, X, *de exceptionibus*, II, 25; *Comp. II*, II, 16, 1; JL, n. 17649.

[29] C. 3, X, *de exceptionibus*, II, 25; *Comp. III*, II, 16, 2; Potthast, *Regesta Pontificum Romanorum inde ab a. post Christum natum 1198 ad a. 1304* (2 vols. in 1, Berolini, 1874-1875), n. 41 (hereafter cited by name of editor).

[30] C. 4, X, *de exceptionibus*, II, 25; *Comp. III*, II, 16, 3; Potthast, n. 2350.

void.[81] On September 1 of the same year he also decreed that the exception against a false witness could be placed after the sentence as well as before.[82]

On August 3, 1209, he ordained that the defendant was not presumed to make a confession of the facts contained in the exceptions when they were proposed. In the same decretal he enacted that the *exceptio falsi* (against witnesses, procurators, instruments of any type) could be placed not only before the sentence but also up to twenty years after the sentence.[83]

On June 3, 1199, Innocent III indicated that it was the ordinary mode of procedure to propose dilatory exceptions before the joinder of issue.[84]

Certain other laws regarding exceptions were made during the pontificate of the same Pope, the exact date of which are not given. He retained the principle of the *exceptio spolii* when he pointed out: "Spoliatus ante restitutionem non cogatur ullatenus respondere." [85] He declared that an excommunicate, or a conspirator, or one living in public concubinage could not introduce a suit in court.[86] He pointed out that failure to mention the cause of removal or of excommunication would render a rescript invalid and require the restitution of a benefice.[87] He decreed that an excommunicated person had the right to place exceptions, to appeal, and to use every type of defense. He said that such a person was especially admitted to the right of placing an exception against a suspected judge.[88] He further pointed out that a replication of minor excommunication placed against the defendant by the plaintiff did not take away the effect of an exception of a major excommunication placed against the plaintiff by the defendant, indicating that one bound by the

[81] C. 4, X, *de procuratoribus,* I, 38; *Comp. III,* I, 22, 1; Potthast, n. 2995.

[82] C. 9, X, *de probationibus,* II, 19; *Comp. III,* II, 11, 4; Potthast, n. 3170.

[83] C. 6, X, *de exceptionibus,* II, 25; *Comp. IV,* II, 5, un.; Potthast, n. 3791.

[84] C. 20, X, *de sententia et re iudicata,* II, 27; *Comp. III,* 18, 10; Potthast, n. 730.

[85] C. 2, X, *de ordine cognitionum,* II, 10.

[86] C. 20, X, *de accusationibus,* V, 1; *Comp. IV,* V, 1, 1.

[87] C. 26, X, *de rescriptis,* I, 3; *Comp. IV,* 1, 2, 3; Potthast, n. 5026.

[88] C. 5, X, *de exceptionibus,* II, 25; *Comp. IV,* II, 1, 2.

minor excommunication was removed from the right to receive the sacraments, while the one bound by the major excommunication was removed from the body of the faithful. This was done to avoid difficulties arising from the fact that the defendant might have talked with a plaintiff bound by a major excommunication before the trial, thereby incurring a minor excommunication himself.[39]

On July 15, 1223, Honorius III (1216-1227) added to the law of exceptions when he declared that one who was acting in defense of the church of which he was in charge could place the exception of excommunication or any other legitimate exception without danger of being affected by the plaintiff's replication of excommunication (even major).[40]

Gregory IX (1227-1234) reiterated the principle that a person could be repelled from pressing his action by virtue of the *exceptio spolii.* The defendant was not required to respond until the restitution had taken place.[41]

He also declared that the exceptions of prescription, previous transaction or *res iudicata* would be valid only if they were true at the time of the trial. If a man was in possession before the trial and lost the claim to this possession at any time before or during the trial he could not claim the exception which corresponded to a *litis finitae.*[42]

Regarding the exception of excommunication, Gregory IX declared that this exception could be placed in any part of the trial.[43] He also pointed out that a defendant was able to place an exception if the cause of the action was not mentioned in the libellus.[44]

Gregory IX also indicated that trials were not to be held on Sundays and Holydays, even with the consent of the parties. This gave rise to the possibility of placing an exception against the time of the trial.[45]

[39] C. 2, X, *de exceptionibus,* II, 25; *Comp. III,* II, 16, 1.
[40] C. 8, X, *de exceptionibus,* II, 25; *Comp. V,* II, 16, 4.
[41] C. 4, X, *de ordine cognitionum,* II, 10.
[42] C. 13, X, *de exceptionibus,* II, 25.
[43] C. 12, X, *de exceptionibus,* II, 25.
[44] C. 3, X, *de libelli oblatione,* III, 3; Potthast, n. 9588.
[45] C. 5, X, *de feriis,* II, 9; Potthast, n. 9592.

Pope Innocent IV (1243-1254) issued a very significant piece of legislation at the I General Council of Lyons in 1245 when he published a decree which contained the following points concerning exceptions:

(a) That the defendant was to name the type of excommunication, and the name of the person who inflicted the penalty, within eight days after claiming this exception; otherwise he would incur the expenses caused the plaintiff by the delay.

(b) That the defendant could use this type of defense only on two occasions, unless a different excommunication were involved, or unless an immediate proof of the same excommunication were forthcoming.

(c) That this exception, placed after the sentence, could suspend the sentence.

(d) That after the excommunication was proved, this exception would hold only until the plaintiff obtained absolution, and should this happen, the trial was to proceed.

(e) That the judge, *ex officio*, was to reject a publicly excommunicated person from the right to sue.[46]

He also declared that peremptory exceptions which did not concern a matter which had been decided previously did not impede the joinder of issue.[47]

Pope Boniface VIII (1294-1303) decreed that the peremptory *exceptio litis finitae*, whether the matter had been determined by an ecclesiastical or civil court, was admissible in Church courts.[48]

Pope Clement V (1305-1314) indicated that the exception of excommunication was to be admitted in any part of the trial, and that no limitation was to be imposed by the judge with regard to the time for proposing this exception.[49]

[46] C. 1, *de exceptionibus*, II, 12, in VI°.

[47] C. 1, *de litis contestatione*, III, 3, in VI°.

[48] C. 2, *de exceptionibus*, II, 12, in VI°.

[49] C. un., *de exceptionibus*, II, 10, in Clem.

CHAPTER III

RULES FOR PLACING EXCEPTIONS

ARTICLE 1. PEREMPTORY EXCEPTIONS

ORDINARILY peremptory exceptions are to be proposed after the joinder of issue unless they are of the *litis finitae* category.[1] Since a peremptory exception consists of an exclusion of an action on its merits and since the action is not properly determined until the joinder of issue, the usual procedure is to propose peremptory exceptions after the issue has been joined.[2] Exceptions which are not of the *litis finitae* type attack the action directly, and it would be useless to attempt to prove them until after the plaintiff has established his intention and presented proofs for it.[3] Moreover, there would be no point to the defendant's proving the exception if the plaintiff does not prove his action for *actore non probante, reus absolvitur.*[4]

Among those which follow this ordinary procedure are the simple peremptory exceptions of prescription, fraud, fear, error, and pleas of fulfilled or invalid contracts.[5] They are to be settled according to the rules for incidental questions.[6]

[1] Canon 1629, c. 1, *de litis contestatione,* II, 3, in VI°; Pirhing, lib. II, tit. VI, nn, 23, 24; Zoesius, lib. II, tit. XXV, n. 6; Schmalzgrueber, lib. II, tit. XXV, n. 23; Reiffenstuel, lib. II, tit. XXV, n. 44; Bouix, *De Iudiciis Ecclesiasticis,* II, 173; Smith, *Elements of Ecclesiastical Law,* II, 201; Coronata, *Institutiones,* n. 1156; Noval, *De Iudiciis,* n. 223; Augustine (Bachofen), *A Commentary on Canon Law,* Vol. VII, *Ecclesiastical Trials* (3. ed., St. Louis: Herder, 1930), 78, 79; Vermeersch-Creusen, *Epitome,* III, n. 68; De Meester, *Compendium,* n. 1550.

[2] Schmalzgrueber, lib. II, tit. XXV, n. 23; Reiffenstuel, lib. II, tit. XXV, n. 45; Bouix, *De Iudiciis Ecclesiasticis,* II, 173; Smith, *Elements of Ecclesiastical Law,* II, 201; Wernz, *Ius Decretalium,* V, n. 419.

[3] Coronata, *Institutiones,* n. 1156; Noval, *De Iudiciis,* n. 223.

[4] Canon 1748.

[5] Noval, *De Iudiciis,* n. 223; Coronata, *Institutiones,* n. 1156.

[6] Canons 1629, § 2; 1633.

Exceptions of the *litis finitae* category are to be proposed and proved before the joinder of issue,[7] since these exceptions impede the joinder of issue.[8] They are classified in this fashion if the issue has already been determined in some way, e.g., by a previous judgment, compromise, etc.[9]

A question that has already been decided cannot be a matter for a new trial; but the trial begins with the joinder of issue; [10] therefore a question decided previously must be considered before the joinder of issue.

Those who maliciously postpone the placing of these exceptions are responsible for any expenses incurred by the plaintiff as a result of their malice.[11] Exceptions of this kind that are proposed later are to be admitted, but definite proof must be brought forth that there is no malice involved in the postponement.[12]

A simple oath, as in the case of dilatory exceptions,[13] will not suffice to guarantee good will, but solid proofs must establish the fact that malice did not provoke the postponement.[14]

After the sentence has been handed down peremptory exceptions cannot be proposed in the same instance; they may be admitted in the instance of appeal, however.[15]

Article 2. Dilatory Exceptions

Ordinarily, dilatory exceptions are to be placed in the beginning of the trial before the joinder of issue.[16] The reason given is that

[7] Canon 1629.

[8] Cc. 1, 2, *de litis contestatione,* II, 3, in VI°; Schmalzgrueber, lib. II, tit. XXV, n. 23; Reiffenstuel, lib. II, tit. XXV, n. 50; Wernz, *Ius Decretalium,* V, n. 419.

[9] Coronata, *Institutiones,* n. 1156.

[10] Noval, *De Iudiciis,* n. 223.

[11] Canon 1629.

[12] Canon 1629.

[13] Canon 1628, § 1.

[14] Coronata, *Institutiones,* n. 1156; Roberti, *De Processibus,* n. 175.

[15] Roberti, *loc. cit.*

[16] Canon 1628, § 1; *Dict. Grat.* p.c. 2, C. III, q. 6; c. 20, X, *de sententia et re iudicata,* II, 27; Barbosa, lib. II, tit. XXV, n. 3; Zoesius, lib. II, tit. XXV,

exceptions of this kind impede the joining of the issue, and if they are not alleged before this time they are considered to have been renounced.[17] This is especially true of the exceptions invoked against the personnel of the court and the method of procedure.[18] For example, the following exceptions should be placed at this time, viz., that the judge is incompetent,[19] suspect [20] or excommunicated; [21] that the plaintiff has no right to sue because he is excommunicated,[22] or because he is a religious,[23] a minor,[24] a prodigal or weak-minded person; [25] that the procurator is not qualified,[26] or does not have a legitimate mandate; [27] that the auditor,[28] the promoter of justice or the defender of the bond are suspect [29] or excommunicated; [30] that the libellus is premature on account of an agreement not to sue for a certain period; [31] that the libellus is not properly drawn up, failing to express for what purpose, against whom and by what right the action is introduced; [32] that the citation is not legal, because it does not

n. 5; Pirhing, lib. II, tit. XXV, n. 18; Schmalzgrueber, lib. II, tit. XXV, n. 20; Reiffenstuel, lib. II, tit. XXV, n. 23; Bouix, *De Iudiciis Ecclesiasticis,* II, 171; Smith, *Elements of Ecclesiastical Law,* II, 199; Wernz, *Ius Decretalium,* V, n. 416; Roberti, *De Processibus,* n. 175; Noval, *De Iudiciis,* n. 222; Vermeersch-Creusen, *Epitome,* III, n. 68; Coronata, *Institutiones,* n. 1800.

[17] Schmalzgrueber, lib. II, tit. XXV, n. 20; Wernz, *Ius Decretalium,* V, n. 416; Lega-Bartoccetti, *Commentarius in Iudicia Ecclesiastica Iuxta Codicem Iuris Canonici* (3 vols., Romae; Anomina Libraria Cattolica Italiana, 1938-1941), I, 258 (hereafter cited *Commentarius*).

[18] Canon 1628, § 1.

[19] Canons 1610; 1611.

[20] Canon 1614.

[21] Canons 2263; 2264; 1892, 1°.

[22] Canons 2263; 1654.

[23] Canon 1652.

[24] Canon 1648.

[25] Canon 1650.

[26] Canons 1657; 1658.

[27] Canon 1659.

[28] Canon 1614, § 1.

[29] Canon 1614, § 3.

[30] Canon 2263.

[31] Noval, *De Iudiciis,* n. 222.

[32] Canon 1708.

have the seal of the court, or that it does not express the cause, the place and date of the trial.[33]

Exemptions from the general rule are granted in several instances:

(1) If something new arises after the joinder of issue which constitutes a dilatory exception, it may be admitted.[34] It is possible that a condition may appear which did not exist before the joinder of issue, v.g., if the judge or other personnel of the court enter into a business relationship with the plaintiff after the trial is under way.[35]

(2) If an exception admissible before the joinder of issue becomes known only after that time, it is to be admitted provided that the defendant seals with an oath the fact that he did not know of the exception before.[36]

(3) An exception against a false procurator may be placed not only after the joinder of issue but also after the sentence.[37] The same is to be said of an exception against a judge who is absolutely incompetent.[38] These two exceptions are valid in any part of the process, from the time before the joinder of issue up to and after the final sentence in the first and in any higher instance,[39] because the sentence and acts upon which the sentence is based labor under an irremediable nullity,[40] which fact can be proposed as an exception perpetually.[41]

(4) Another notable exemption from the general rule as to the time for placing dilatory exceptions is the exception of excommuni-

[33] Canon 1715.

[34] Canon 1628, § 1; c. 4, X, *de exceptionibus,* II, 25; Reiffenstuel, lib. II, tit. XXV, n. 33; Pirhing, lib. II, tit. XXV, n. 27; Bouix, *De Iudiciis Ecclesiasticis,* II, 172; Wernz, *Ius Decretalium,* V, n. 416.

[35] Noval, *De Iudiciis,* n. 222.

[36] Canon 1628, § 1; c. 4, X, *de exceptionibus,* II, 25; Bouix, *De Iudiciis Ecclesiasticis,* II, 172.

[37] Canon 1892, n. 3; c. 4, X, *de procuratoribus,* I, 38; Zoesius, lib. II, tit. XXV, n. 5; Pirhing, lib. II, tit. XXV, n. 28; Schmalzgrueber, lib. II, tit. XXV, n. 22.

[38] Canons 1628, § 2; 1892; 1893; Schmalzgrueber, lib. II, tit. XXV, n. 22; Reiffenstuel, lib. II, tit. XXV, n. 41; Bouix, *De Iudiciis Ecclesiasticis,* II, 173.

[39] Noval, *De Iudiciis,* n. 222.

[40] Canon 1892.

[41] Canon 1893.

cation. This exception, whether it be placed against the judge, the plaintiff, the procurator, auditor, promoter of justice or defender of the bond,[42] may be placed at any time before the definitive sentence.[43]

Noval[44] maintains that this exception may not be placed after the case is appealed, understanding that the definitive sentence is issued in the court of the first instance. Roberti, on the other hand, points out that the definitive sentence is predicated not as of the first instance only but in any stage or hearing of a trial (*quolibet gradu*),[45] indicating that the exception is admissible in the higher instances as well. Król[46] adheres to this opinion of Roberti, pointing out that the term "*gradus*" is a technical term used in the Code to indicate a judicial instance.[47] The writer also adheres to this opinion because of the use of this term as well as the unqualified freedom implied in the use of the accompanying pronominal adjective "*quolibet.*"

The opinion of Roberti is more acceptable also because the purpose of the law is to encourage excommunicated persons to seek absolution from their censure[48] which seeking would be as effectively beneficial in the higher court as it is in the lower. If an excommunicated person saw that he would gain the full rights of a plaintiff by being absolved from his censure hc might take advantage of the opportunity to do so.

(5) Since a sentence which would be pronounced in the cause of a person who lacks juridical capacity would be irremediably null,[49] a useless procedure would be avoided regardless of when the exception is placed. This would serve the interests of justice, since such an invalid sentence could be attacked later by the *querela nullitatis*,[50]

[42] Canons 2263; 2264; 2256, 2°.

[43] Canon 1628, § 3.

[44] *De Iudiciis*, n. 222.

[45] Canon 1628, § 3; Roberti, *De Processibus*, n. 175.

[46] *The Defendant in Contentious Trials*, 109.

[47] Cf. canon 1571.

[48] Roberti, *loc. cit.*

[49] Canon 1892, 3°.

[50] Canons 1892-1897.

or an action based on such a sentence could be nullified by the *exceptio nullitatis*.[51]

(6) An exception against an inept libellus or citation may be placed after the joinder of issue because these are the foundations of the trial, and if the foundation is not sound, the entire structure falls.[52]

Those who use exceptions maliciously by knowingly postponing them without cause will be liable to the expense which may result.[53] A bond deposited before the joinder of issue may be exacted to insure the proper use of the exceptions and to limit unnecessary delays.[54] This law was introduced by the Code to avoid any imposition causing expenses which might easily be avoided.[55]

With regard to the order of placing dilatory exceptions, the exceptions of suspicion and incompetence are to be indicated as early as possible in order to avoid a useless procedure.[56] Other exceptions take the following order: (1) those against the person of the plaintiff and his procurator; (2) those alleged on account of the person of the plaintiff himself; (3) those concerning the time and place of the trial; (4) those concerning the libellus.[57]

[51] Canons 1892-1893.

[52] Schmalzgrueber, lib. II, tit. XXV, n. 26; Bouix, *De Iudiciis Ecclesiasticis,* II, 173; Roberti, *De Processibus,* n. 175.

[53] Roberti, *De Processibus,* n. 175.

[54] Canons 1631; 1788.

[55] Roberti, *loc. cit.*

[56] Hostiensis, *Summa Aurea,* f. 181v; Schmalzgrueber, lib. II, tit. XXV, n. 20; Wernz, *Ius Decretalium,* V, n. 418.

[57] Schmalzgrueber, lib. II, tit. XXV, n. 20; Wernz, *Ius Decretalium,* V, n. 418; The Code and post-Code authors are silent about this order.

CHAPTER IV

THE SETTLEMENT OF EXCEPTIONS

ARTICLE 1. IN FIRST INSTANCE

SPECIFIC provision for the settlement of exceptions is given by the Code only in one instance. Canon 1629, § 2, points out that peremptory exceptions which are not of the *litis finitae* category are proposed after the joinder of issue and settled according to the rules for incidental questions. It seems that all the exceptions should follow this same method of settlement, since an exception may be identified as an incidental question. The latter is defined as something proposed after the trial has begun. Although it is not contained in the libellus, it so pertains to the cause that it ought to be settled before the principal issue is considered.[1]

Exceptions partake of these aspects, since they may delay the trial, bar action or quash the cause, thereby affecting the principal issue in an intimate way.[2] They will not be contained in the original libellus because they are instruments of defense,[3] the original libellus being the bill of complaint issued by the plaintiff.[4]

Presupposed, then, that all exceptions follow the method of incidental questions, they may be proposed either orally or in writing by means of a separate libellus.[5] If they are proposed orally they should be registered in the acts.[6]

[1] Canon 1837; Coronata, *Institutiones*, n. 1369; Roberti, *De Processibus*, II, n. 394; Wernz-Vidal, *Ius Canonicum*, VI, n. 545.

[2] Wernz, *Ius Decretalium*, V, n. 411; Roberti, *De Processibus*, II, n. 273; Noval, *De Iudiciis*, n. 299; Coronata, *Institutiones*, n. 1195; Vermeersch-Creusen, *Epitome*, III, n. 68.

[3] Lega, *De Iudiciis Ecclesiasticis*, I, n. 170; Wernz, *Ius Decretalium*, V, n. 410; De Meester, *Compendium*, n. 1561; Roberti, *De Processibus*, n. 272.

[4] Canon 1706.

[5] Canon 1838.

[6] Cf. canon 1707, § 1.

As far as possible, the general rules for introducing the principal cause are also to be observed in introducing the exception,[7] with less rigor, however.[8] The libellus containing the exception should contain the name of the judge or of the tribunal before which it is being introduced, the object and purpose of the exception and the name of the person or persons against whom it is made. It should also specify the rights upon which it is based. It is to be signed by the one proposing it, with the day, month, year and place indicated.[9]

After the libellus is legitimately proposed according to the time and manner for placing exceptions,[10] the judge having conducted a separate hearing, with the promoter of justice or defender of the bond present, if necessary,[11] should either accept or reject the petition. If it pertains to the principal issue he should accept it; if it does not, he should reject it with a decree.[12]

Roberti [13] maintains that the petition should be examined by the principal judge unless the *iudex instructor* should consider the matter of little importance. Noval [14] on the other hand, indicates that the auditor or the judge delegated to draw up the process may rule on the petition just as the presiding judge of a collegiate tribunal.

Noval's opinion seems more acceptable, because if a judge is qualified to handle any part of an important legal procedure he should be deemed qualified to handle the whole process unless limitations are imposed upon him by the one delegating. Moreover, the law does not distinguish.[15]

Even if this libellus is rejected unjustly by the judge an appeal strictly so called is not given to the injured party unless the decree

[7] Canons 1706-1725; cf. canon 1838.

[8] Coronata, *Institutiones*, n. 1370.

[9] Cf. canon 1708.

[10] Canons 1628; 1629.

[11] The promoter of justice would be present in causes affecting the public welfare, and the defender of the bond in causes concerning sacred ordination or matrimony. Cf. canon 1586.

[12] Canon 1839.

[13] *De Processibus*, n. 396.

[14] *De Iudiciis*, n. 579.

[15] Canon 1839.

has the effect of a definitive sentence, or the appeal is combined with an appeal against the definitive sentence.[16]

If the libellus is accepted, the exception is to be decided in a judicial form or by a mere decree according to the quality and gravity of the matter in question.[17] If the exception would involve a matter of great importance or require extensive proofs and a number of witnesses, the judicial form should be observed. If the question may be solved easily, or if it be of little importance, or if the parties so agree, the extrajudicial form may be used.[18] Even if the judicial form has not been followed, the reasons for the decision, as based on law and fact, should be indicated in the decree.[19]

If it is decided that the judicial form is to be observed, the ordinary rules for judicial procedure are to be followed, but the judge must see that the delays are as short as possible.[20] A separate joinder of issue, preparing of the cause, conclusion and decision, all in shortened form, will be necessary.[21]

If there is only one judge, then the deciding of the question and the handing down of sentence rests with him.[22] If a collegiate tribunal is hearing the cause [23] all of the judges will submit their conclusions on the merits of the question indicating their reasons based on fact and law for their decision. This will take place at a meeting called for that purpose. The conclusions are to be included in the acts of the cause, with strict secrecy being observed, however, as to their contents. After a discussion of the question, led by the presid-

[16] Canons 1880, 6°; 1610, § 3; 1612, sq.; Lega, *De Iudiciis Ecclesiasticis*, n. 560; Coronata, *Institutiones*, n. 1371; Noval, *De Iudiciis*, n. 579; Roberti, *De Processibus*, II, n. 397. A decree has the effect of a definitive sentence if it so affects the sentence that the latter cannot stand without the former. Cf. Coronata, *Institutiones*, n. 1372, Roberti, *De Processibus*, n. 397.

[17] Canon 1840, § 1.

[18] Wernz-Vidal, *Ius Canonicum*, VI, n. 548; Coronata, *Institutiones*, n. 1372.

[19] Canon 1840, § 3.

[20] Canon 1840, § 2. Cf. canons 1706-1725.

[21] Roberti, *De Processibus*, II, n. 397; Coronata, *Institutiones*, n. 1372.

[22] Canon 1872.

[23] Canon 1576.

ing judge, the majority opinion will be written into the form of a sentence by the *ponens*.[24]

When it can be done conveniently, the same rules are to be observed in constructing the interlocutory sentence as hold when the definitive sentence is produced.[25] The judge is to decide whether the rules of constructing the definitive sentence are to be observed.[26] According to Coronata, if the interlocutory sentence has the force of a definitive sentence, the same rules are to be observed in constructing the former as in constructing the latter; if otherwise, they are to be limited accordingly.[27] This opinion, however, seems to go beyond the law and take the discretionary faculty away from the judge. The writer holds that the judge may determine that the rules for the definitive sentence may be observed even though the interlocutory sentence does not have the force of a definitive sentence, for it is within the province of the judge to decide matters of this kind.

If the rules for the definitive sentence are observed in their entirety, the following form and order will be employed: (1) the sentence will begin with the invocation of the name of God; (2) then follow the names of the judges or the tribunal, the names of the plaintiff, of the defendant, and of the procurators, with their domiciles, the names of the promoter of justice, of the defender of the bond and of those who have a part in the trial; (3) next, a brief resumé of the case involved in the exception with the conclusions of the parties will be contained therein; (4) then the dispositive part follows with the reasons for the sentence preceding; (5) it is closed with the indication of the date and place of publication along with the signatures of the judge or judges and the notary.[28]

Noval [29] suggests that the invocation of the divine name, the names of the personnel of the court, of the parties and of the procurators may be omitted in the interlocutory sentence, probably because these will be contained in the definitive sentence. He also

[24] Canons 1872; 1871; 1577, § 1; 1584.

[25] Canon 1875.

[26] Coronata, *Institutiones*, n. 1402.

[27] *Loc. cit.*

[28] Canon 1874.

[29] *De Iudiciis*, nn. 629, 630.

maintains that the facts of the question may be restricted to the details which establish a relationship to the principal cause. The dispositive part along with the basis in law and fact seem to be essential, however, and the indication of the date and signatures seem to be necessary adjuncts. The discretion of the judge, however, will determine the entire matter.

The following formula for the interlocutory sentence is suggested by Lemieux: [30]

N. .... vs. N. ....

p. ....
(natura processus)
n. ....

Sententia Interlocutoria
In Nomine Dei. Amen.

1. (Hic habetur brevis relatio quaestionis incidentis agitatae et conclusionum partium.)
2. (Hic sequitur motivatio.)
   In iure ....
   In facto ....
3. (Hic datur pars dispositiva.)
   Quibus omnibus tum in iure cum in facto perpensis, Nos, infrascripti Iudices, declaramus ....
4. (Concluditur cum indicatione diei et loci cum subscriptione omnium iudicum et notarii.)

Article 2. Appeals

An appeal consists of the invoking of the aid of a superior court in order to secure redress against an injury or grievance, either already inflicted or about to be inflicted by an inferior judge.[31] If the sentence pronounced on the suit in question by the judge of an

[30] *The Sentence in Ecclesiastical Procedure,* The Catholic University of America Canon Law Studies, n. 87 (Washington, D. C.: The Catholic University of America, 1934), p. 88.

[31] Schmalzgrueber, lib. II, tit. XXVIII, n. 1; Connolly, *Appeals,* The Catholic University of America Canon Law Studies, n. 79 (Washington, D. C.: The Catholic University of America, 1932), p. 3.

inferior court is not considered just, an appeal to a superior tribunal is allowed to all parties concerned.[82]

The fact of whether or not an exception will be admitted as the basis for an appeal will depend largely on the consideration of Canon 1880, 6°. According to the norm therein indicated, a decree or interlocutory sentence which does not have the force of a definitive sentence cannot be appealed unless it is joined with an appeal from the definitive sentence. Ordinarily, decrees may not be appealed because they usually concern matters of little importance.[83] However, if the decree should put an end to the trial, an appeal will be admitted.[84]

The following instances of an interlocutory sentence having the effect of a definitive sentence are indicated by Connolly: [85] "When the interlocutory sentence defines one article of the principal cause; when it relieves a judge of further participation in the cause; when it admits or rejects a peremptory exception; when it imposes an obligation on one of the parties that cannot be remedied or corrected by the definitive sentence; and finally, when it is of such a nature that it so defines a point or question raised in the trial that the entire proceedings are thereby terminated, thus rendering a definitive sentence on the principal cause unnecessary." [86]

What Connolly states about peremptory exceptions being the basis of an appeal is true with regard to simple peremptory exceptions, for these concern the merits of the case and invariably will be identified with the principal cause in such a way that they will influence the definitive sentence. However, the writer holds that

[82] Wernz-Vidal, *Ius Canonicum,* VI, n. 602; Noval, *De Iudiciis,* n. 643; Roberti, *De Processibus,* II, n. 468; Vermeersch-Creusen, *Epitome,* III, n. 237; Blat, *Commentarium Textus Codicis Iuris Canonici, Liber IV, De Processibus* (Romae: Collegio Angelico, 1927), n. 409; Cocchi, *Commentarium in Codicem Iuris Canonici* (8 vols., Turin: 1925-1927), *De Processibus,* n. 223; Schmalzgrueber, lib. II, tit. XXVIII, n. 7; Reiffenstuel, lib. II, tit. XXVIII, n. 32; Bouix, *De Iudiciis Ecclesiasticis,* II, 248; Lega, *De Iudiciis Ecclesiasticis,* I, n. 629; Connolly, *Appeals,* p. 63.

[83] Connolly, *Appeals,* p. 79.

[84] Canon 1880, 6°.

[85] *Appeals,* pp. 69, 70.

[86] Cf. Reiffenstuel, lib. II, tit. XXVIII, n. 18, sq.; Wernz-Vidal, *Ius Canonicum,* VI, n. 606.

the same cannot be said of peremptory exceptions of the *litis finitae* category. A sentence that has become a *res iudicata* may not be appealed,[37] because litigation should not be protracted unduly.[38] Therefore, if the exception *res iudicata* is registered against a plaintiff by the defendant, the plaintiff may not register an appeal from the sentence ruling on this exception. The extraordinary remedies against the *res iudicata* will be considered below, when that exception is treated *in specie*. Nor may a sentence pronounced as a result of a decisory oath be appealed.[39] If an exception based on the fact that a decisory oath was taken confirming certain alleged facts [40] an appeal for or against the exception will not be admitted. The original oath must have been definitive in character inasmuch as it must have been decisive in its effect.[41] This exception cannot be appealed because the decisory oath has the effect of a *res iudicata*.[42]

The same may be said of the *litis finitae* exceptions of compromise and arbitration because these also have the effect of a *res iudicata*.[43] Therefore all exceptions of the *litis finitae* category may not be attacked by the ordinary remedy of appeal; the extraordinary remedies of *oppositio tertii*,[44] *restitutio in integrum*,[45] or *querela nullitatis* [46] must be employed.

Although only a formally valid sentence is admitted as the basis for an appeal,[47] some injustice may have been present in the pronouncing of the sentence. This may have resulted from error, ignorance or prejudice, wrong legal applications, reliance on non-existing

[37] Canon 1880, 4°.

[38] Coronata, *Institutiones*, n. 1423; Roberti, *De Processibus*, n. 508; Wernz-Vidal, *Ius Canonicum*, VI, n. 635.

[39] Canon 1880, 5°.

[40] This exception will be considered further in the treatment of exceptions *in specie*.

[41] Canon 1880, 5°.

[42] Canon 1834, cf. Wernz, *Ius Decretalium*, V, n. 645; Coronata, *Institutiones*, II, n. 1466; Noval, *De Iudiciis*, n. 573; Roberti, *De Processibus*, n. 389.

[43] C. 1, X, *de transactionibus*, I, 36; Wernz, *Ius Decretalium*, V, n. 46; Noval, *De Iudiciis*, n. 721; Coronata, *Institutiones*, n. 1446.

[44] Canons 1898-1901.

[45] Canons 1905-1907.

[46] Canons 1679-1683.

[47] Canon 1880, 3°.

law, lack of evidence, unwarranted sentence, etc.[48] Only sound and basic reasons will permit the appeal. However, the benefit of doubt about the character of the reasons advanced is to be given to the one appealing.[49]

Therefore, if the decision on the exception is embodied in a decree or interlocutory sentence which has the force of a definitive sentence, or if the appeal based on the exception is joined with the appeal from the definitive sentence, it will be admitted in the instance of appeal.[50]

Particular provision for the exception of suspicion is provided in the Code as far as appeal is concerned. No appeal is permitted when the law requires a speedy settlement of a matter in question; [51] but the law requires a speedy settlement of the exception of suspicion; [52] therefore no appeal based on this exception will be admitted.

An appeal from an invalid sentence will not be admitted.[53] Therefore, if an exception is placed against a judge because he is absolutely incompetent,[54] or against a collegiate tribunal because it does not have the required number of judges,[55] or against a plaintiff because he does not have the right to stand in judgment,[56] or against a procurator who does not have a proper mandate,[57] and if such an exception is disregarded by the judge, the one registering the exception may not institute an appeal,[58] but must employ the *querela nullitatis.*[59]

Article 3. Proof of an Exception

When a defendant proposes an exception he thereby becomes the *actor* or the plaintiff in regard to the burden of proof, although

[48] Connolly, *Appeals*, p. 70.
[49] Wernz-Vidal, *Ius Canonicum,* VI, n. 610.
[50] Canon 1880, 6°.
[51] Canon 1880, 7°.
[52] Canon 1616.
[53] Canon 1880, 3°.
[54] Canons 1611-1613; 1892, 1°.
[55] Canons 1576, § 1; 1892, 1°.
[56] Canons 1646; 1654, 1892, 2°.
[57] Canons 1655-1666; 1892, 3°.
[58] Canon 1880, 3°.
[59] Canon 1892.

not in respect to anything else. This means that the one proposing the exception takes upon himself the obligation of proving the exception he has proposed.[60]

The manner of proving an exception will necessarily differ according to the type of exception proposed. Thus in the dilatory exceptions of incompetency, suspicion and excommunication the proof will be concerned with external facts. So too in the peremptory exceptions of *litis finitae* and of prescription. The exception of fraud can also often be proved by external indications. In the cases of fear and simple error, however, the defendant is often confronted with a singularly difficult task. These two, fear and error, being essentially interior may at times be very difficult to demonstrate. In all cases of alleged fear or error, considerable importance must be attached to the testimony of the defendant proposing the exception. Consequently his character and reputation for veracity will have to be carefully weighed in judgment. The mere word of the one alleging fear or error is never sufficient to establish full proof for the exception. Rather his testimony must be corroborated to a greater or lesser extent by the deposition of others or by convincing external signs indicating at least the probability of such fear or error.[61]

If there is incomplete proof and the defendant proposing the exception has no further means available to strengthen his assertion, the judge may order or admit (if requested) the taking of an oath to supplement the proofs.[62] This is termed a supplementary or suppletory oath, and it can be asked or admitted in those cases wherein the right or affair or the fact involved is not of great importance and when this right, affair or fact is proper to the one taking the suppletory oath.[63]

[60] This was the same in Roman Law. Cf. D. (44.1) 1.

[61] For the requisites of proof of fear in the matrimonial consent, cf. Sipos, *Enchiridion Iuris Canonici* (ed. altera, Pécs: "Haladás R.T.," 1931), p. 587.

[62] Canon 1829. For the requisites of a suppletory oath, the procedure in administering it, and its effects, cf. Moriarty, *Oaths in Ecclesiastical Courts,* The Catholic University of America Canon Law Studies, n. 110 (Washington, D. C.: The Catholic University of America, 1937), pp. 66-80.

[63] Canon 1830, § 2.

CHAPTER V

LITIS FINITAE EXCEPTIONS

EXCEPTIONS of the *litis finitae* category will not permit the introduction of the suit because the issue has already been decided in some fashion. When an exception of this type is presented the judge will consider the validity of the facts upon which the exception is based, whether or not the facts of the exception are identical with the issue involved in the new suit, and whether or not the cause of pleading and the same condition of persons concur in both instances. When the identity is established the judge will set aside the action and bar further suit. Exceptions of this type should be placed before the joinder of issue in order to avoid a useless procedure.[1]

ARTICLE 1. *Res Iudicata*

A *res iudicata* may be defined as a valid sentence which, as such, can no longer be attacked by the ordinary remedy of appeal.[2] Since it is the essential purpose of the judicial process to render a question definitively and permanently adjudicated[3] so that litigation may not be protracted unduly,[4] the term *res iudicata* is applied to

[1] Canon 1629, § 1.

[2] Feeney, *Restititio in Integrum,* The Catholic University of America Canon Law Studies, n. 129 (Washington, D. C.: The Catholic University of America, Press, 1941), 95; Vermeersch-Creusen, *Epitome,* III, n. 245; Noval, *De Iudiciis,* n. 672; Coronata, *Institutiones,* n. 1423; Roberti, *De Processibus,* nn. 243, 508; Lemieux, *The Sentence in Ecclesiastical Procedure,* 101; Muñiz, *Procedimientos Eclesiásticos* (2. ed., 3 vols., Sevilla: Lib. de Sobrino de Izquierdo, 1926), III, n. 516; Wernz-Vidal, *Ius Canonicum,* VI, nn. 631, 632.

[3] Canons 1552; 1873, § 1; 1902-1904; 17, § 3.

[4] Coronata, *Institutiones,* n. 1423; Roberti, *De Processibus,* II, n. 508; Wernz-Vidal, *Ius Canonicum,* VI, n. 635.

causes which are not to be reconsidered unless extraordinary circumstances so warrant.[5] It is ordinarily to be presumed that the judges have done their duty in deciding the issue, hence leaving no need for reconsideration of the case, once all the ordinary legal means have been exhausted.[6]

A *res iudicata* is arrived at in three ways, viz.: (1) by a second conformable sentence; (2) by failure to appeal within the time stated by law or by abandoning an appeal already instituted; (3) by a single definitive sentence when the law does not grant an appeal.[7]

There are some sentences which do not achieve the status of a *res iudicata*. These concern causes dealing with the state of persons.[8] Of this category are causes regarding the matrimonial bond, religious profession or the clerical state.[9] Even these causes should not be readmitted after a second conformable sentence unless sound reasons for so doing are indicated.[10]

Pre-Code law and jurisprudence were more extensive in the definition of causes which did not achieve the status of the *res iudicata*.

[5] The extraordinary remedies against the *res iudicata* are the *oppositio tertii* (when a third party is injured by the sentence—canons 1898-1901) the *restitutio in integrum* (when natural equity demands a reconsideration of the cause from the beginning in the case of a person who has been injured by a valid but rescissible act—canons 1905-1907; cf. Feeney, *Restitutio in Integrum*, p. 49); and the *querela nullitatis* (when an act or contract is null—canons 1679-1683). Cf. Vermeersch-Creusen, *Epitome*, III, nn. 105-108, 116-121, 243; Roberti, *De Processibus*, n. 508; Muñiz, *Procedimientos Eclesiásticos*, III, n. 516; Wernz-Vidal, *Ius Canonicum*, VI, nn. 631, 632.

[6] Coronata, *Institutiones*, n. 1423; Roberti, *De Processibus*, n. 508; Wernz-Vidal, *Ius Canonicum*, VI, n. 635.

[7] Canons 1902; 1880. Cf. Muñiz, *Procedimientos Eclesiásticos*, III, n. 516; Roberti, *De Processibus*, II, n. 510; Wernz-Vidal, *Ius Canonicum*, VI, n. 533; cc. 13, 15, X, *de sententia et re iudicata*, II, 27; Schmalzgrueber, lib. II, tit. XXVII, n. 63; De Angelis, *Praelectiones Iuris Canonici ad methodum Decretalium Gregorii IX exactae* (9 vols., Romae, 1877-1891), lib. II, tit. XXVII, p. 246 (hereafter cited *Praelectiones*).

[8] Canon 1903.

[9] Coronata, *Institutiones*, n. 1424; Muñiz, *Procedimientos Eclesiásticos*, III, n. 517, p. 441; Noval, *De Iudiciis*, n. 675.

[10] Canon 1903.

In addition to matrimonial causes regarding the bond of marriage,[11] causes regarding censures,[12] causes concerning benefices whose sentences were prejudicial to the Church or to souls,[13] causes whose sentences were based on false instruments or testimony,[14] and condemnatory sentences in criminal causes could not become *res iudicatae* before the Code.[15]

Among the effects of the *res iudicata* is that it creates a *presumptio iuris et de iure* in favor of the victorious party.[16] This implies that the sentence cannot be attacked again directly. Indirect proofs, however, which destroy the foundation of the presumption, may constitute the basis for reconsidering the case.[17]

The principal effect of the *res iudicata* for the purpose of this treatise is that it provides a peremptory exception which will impede a further introduction of the same cause.[18] This exception is to be revealed by the judge *ex officio,* since the common good requires that a matter that has been finally adjudicated should not be subjected to a new trial.[19]

In order that the exception of *res iudicata* may be effective three conditions are required, viz.: (1) that the object of the trial be the same; (2) that the cause of pleading be the same; and (3) that

[11] Benedictus XIV, const. *"Dei Miseratione,"* 30 nov. 1741—*Fontes,* n. 318; Benedictus XV, chirographum, *"Attentis expositis,"* 28 iun. 1915—*Fontes,* n. 705.

[12] Pirhing, lib. II, tit. XXVII, n. 58; Schmalzgrueber, lib. II, tit. XXVII, n. 65.

[13] C. 7, X, *de sententia et re iudicata,* II, 27; Schmalzgrueber, lib. II, tit. XXVII, n. 66.

[14] C. 22, X, *de sententia et re iudicata,* II, 27; Schmalzgrueber, lib. II, tit. XXVII, n. 66.

[15] De Angelis, *Praelectiones;* lib. II, tit. XXVII, p. 249.

[16] Canon 1904, § 1; cc. 13, 16, X, *de sententia et re iudicata,* II, 27; Schmalzgrueber, lib. II, tit. XXVII, n. 78; De Angelis, *Praelectiones,* lib. II, tit. XXVII, p. 247.

[17] Canon 1826.

[18] Canon 1904, § 2.

[19] Canon 1742, § 1. Cf. Roberti, *De Processibus,* II, n. 509; Coronata, *Institutiones,* n. 1425.

the same condition of persons concur.[20] If not all of the three conditions prevail, the exception is not verified.[21]

A *res iudicata* may not be used as a basis for gain in favor of or in prejudice to those not concerned in the trial, for a decision is to affect only the litigants, just as a contract affects only those who enter into the contract.[22] When the *res iudicata*, therefore, is lodged against the rights of a third party not concerned in the case, it may not be admitted as a valid exception.[23] This is so because ordinarily the condition of persons involved in the new action does not conform exactly to the requirements just indicated for introducing the exception. Some different circumstances usually prevail in the cause of a third party. On the same basis a third party may not use this

[20] Gonzalez-Tellez, lib. II, tit. XXV, n. 7; Schmalzgrueber, lib. II, tit. XXV, n. 47; Bouix, *De Iudiciis Ecclesiasticis*, II, 177; Coronata, *Institutiones*, n. 1425; Roberti, *De Processibus*, n. 513.

(1) The object of the trial consists of the thing which the action is directed to safeguard. Juridic, not material, identity is considered here. It is possible to have a juridic identity when the things appear to be different externally, v.g., a thing and its price constitute one object, because the denial of one is equivalent to the denial of the other. Cf. Roberti, *De Processibus*, n. 224.

The principle, *pars continetur in toto, et totum in parte non est*, is a basis for determining the identity of an object. If a part is necessarily contained in the whole, it does not constitute a different object from the whole, v.g., if full credit has been denied, a person cannot plead part of the same credit. On the other hand, if some part has been denied, the remaining parts may be different objects. Cf. Roberti, *De Processibus*, n. 224.

(2) A cause of pleading is the juridic fact upon which a right is based, v.g., contract. Cf. Roberti, *loc. cit.*

(3) Persons are considered as having a certain juridic condition or capacity to plead a cause. Several physical persons may have the same juridic condition, v.g., the principal, his heirs, successors and sureties. Also, one physical person may possess several juridic conditions, v.g., a guardian who acts in his own name and in the name of another. The *res iudicata* is concerned only with parties under the same juridic condition. It does not concern third parties unless they participate in the cause and are considered parties to the juridic fact. Cf. Roberti, *De Processibus*, nn. 413, 416, 419, 422.

[21] Coronata, *Institutiones*, n. 1425.

[22] C. 25, X, *de sententia et re iudicata*, II, 27; Schmalzgrueber, lib. II, tit. XXVII, n. 81; canons 17, § 3; 1904, § 2.

[23] Roberti, *De Processibus*, n. 513.

exception against a plaintiff. The remedy of *oppositio tertii* will be available to that party, however.[24]

Exceptions to this rule, however, are had in the case of connected causes or individual causes common to several if they concern the same matter and cause of defense.[25]

The exception of *res iudicata* is admissible even though the decision was rendered by a secular court, in a matter, however, in which it is competent.[26] A cause of this kind was appealed to the Rota and an affirmative decision was given, namely, that "the plea of *res iudicata* based on the judgment in the civil court is a bar to the trial of the same case on its merits in the ecclesiastical court of the first instance." [27]

Since the *res iudicata* is an exception of the *litis finitae* category it should be proposed and proved before the joinder of issue.

It would seem that this exception might be settled by a decree, for the question should be decided easily without extensive proofs and many witnesses.[28] A copy of the previous court sentence ordinarily should be sufficient to settle this exception, unless there is difficulty in deciding the identity of the exception with the cause in question.

Article 2. Compromise

A compromise may be defined as an onerous contract designed to put an end to litigation by which something is given, retained or promised.[29] Its principal purpose is to arrive at a settlement without

[24] Canons 1898-1901.

[25] C. 22, X, *de accusationibus,* V, 1; Schmalzgrueber, lib. II, tit. XXVII, nn. 83, 84; Pirhing, lib. II, tit. XXVII, n. 82; De Angelis, *Praelectiones,* lib. II, tit. XXVII, p. 251.

[26] C. 2, *de exceptionibus,* II, 12, in VI°; Barbosa, lib. II, tit. XXV, n. 1; Pirhing, lib. II, tit. XXV, nn. 39, 40; Schmalzgrueber, lib. II, tit. XXV, nn. 48-50.

[27] *AAS,* XIV (1922), 652.

[28] Muñiz, *Procedimientos Eclesiásticos,* n. 179; Wernz-Vidal, *Ius Canonicum,* VI, n. 548; Coronata, *Institutiones,* III, n. 1372.

[29] Wernz, *Ius Decretalium,* V, n. 34; Coronata, *Institutiones,* n. 1443; Noval, *De Iudiciis,* n. 721.

a trial by effecting an amicable agreement.[30] This effect is called composition or concord.[31]

Only those may enter into a compromise who are capable of making a contract. For instance, those who lack the use of reason would be excluded, because such an action on their part would be opposed to the natural law.[32] Some restrictions are also placed by the positive law, viz., bishops, rectors and administrators must employ the solemnities of alienation in entering into a compromise.[33] Procurators may not make a transaction without a special mandate of the principal.[34]

A compromise is permitted only with regard to those things about which there is a real doubt.[35] If the matter is certain the pact is invalid.[36] If one or the other of the litigants should know that the issue is certain and nevertheless should consent to a compromise he would be bound to restore anything he has received as a result of the compromise.[37]

Criminal causes, spiritual matters, possessory titles of benefices and the bond of marriage are excluded as objects of a compromise.[38]

Criminal causes are excluded because they pertain to the public welfare and cannot be the object of a private settlement.[39] Any bargaining entered into with the delinquent by the promoter of justice would frustrate the purpose of the Church in seeking the former's amendment and the reparation of scandal. The promoter would be abusing his office by such action.[40]

30 Noval, *De Iudiciis*, n. 719.

31 Canon 1928, § 1.

32 Schmalzgrueber, lib. I, tit. XXXV, n. 8; Wernz, *Ius Decretalium*, V, n. 38; Noval, *De Iudiciis*, n. 721.

33 Canon 1927, § 2; 1530-1533; c. 3, X, *de transactionibus*, I, 36; Wernz, *Ius Decretalium*, V, n. 38; Noval, *De Iudiciis*, n. 721; Coronata, *Institutiones*, n. 1445.

34 Canon 1662; c. 4, *de procuratoribus*, I, 49, in VI° Coronata, *Institutiones*, n. 1443; Wernz-Vidal, *Ius Canonicum*, VI, n. 666.

35 Wernz, *Ius Decretalium*, V, n. 39; Noval, *De Iudiciis*, nn. 719, 721.

36 Schmalzgrueber, lib. I, tit. XXXVI, n. 7.

37 Noval, *De Iudiciis*, n. 721.

38 Canon 1927, § 1; cc. 2, 9, 10, X, *de transactionibus*, I, 36.

39 Noval, *ibidem*, n. 723.

40 Noval, *ibidem*, n. 725.

Simony would result from compromises made concerning matters which are either intrinsically spiritual or also only temporal but at the same time inseparably connected with the spiritual, if in either case there should take place a giving, a retaining or a promise of a temporal thing.[41] However, if purely temporal ecclesiastical property is involved, or if the temporal object annexed to the spiritual may be considered and treated separately, v.g., a cemetery, then a transaction may be made provided the requirements for alienation are observed.[42]

Marriage, being indissoluble by virtue of the divine law, cannot be subjected to a compromise. The parties are not capable of renouncing this indissolubility.[43]

Beneficiary matters may not be made the object of a compromise when the possessory title is disputed, and at the same time without the approval of the proper authority, because a benefice pertains to the common good, and therefore a private bargaining may not be permitted to become the basis for a change in its status.[44]

Canon 1926 points out that the civil law of the place where the compromise is entered into is to serve as a norm for the validity of the compromise unless the particular statutes are opposed to the divine or ecclesiastical law, or unless there is a special provision for the question in the Code. In American Civil Law the canonical term compromise is represented by the legal terms *accord* and *satisfaction.*[45]

Certain legal requirements are specified for valid accord according to the Anglo-American Common Law with some additional limitations imposed by the state laws. The Common Law provides that

[41] Canons 727; 1927, § 1.

[42] Canon 1927, § 2; cf. canons 1530-1532.

[43] Coronata, *Institutiones,* n. 1445; cf. canon 1927, § 1.

[44] Wernz, *Ius Decretalium,* V, n. 40; cf. canon 1927, § 1.

[45] The process is described as "an agreement between two parties to give and accept something in satisfaction of a right of action which one has against the other, which when performed is a bar to all actions upon this account." Cf. Bouvier, *Law Dictionary and Concise Encyclopedia* (8. ed., 3. revision by F. Rowle, 3 vols., Kansas City, Mo., 1914), s.v. "Accord and Satisfaction" (hereafter cited *Law Dictionary*).

real actions are excluded; that the accord must give some advantage to the creditor insofar as it should not defeat his claim entirely; that mere payment of part of a debt does not constitute satisfaction, even if it is accepted; that the payment of a part is, however, permitted if the claim is disputed or contingent, or if an additional benefit is received by the creditor; that the terms of the satisfaction be certain and complete.[46]

Generally considered, the principles of the Common Law in this matter hold in all the states. Some specific provisions, however, are indicated in the various statutes. In California, the District of Columbia, Georgia, Kansas, Minnesota, Montana, New Hampshire, North Carolina, North Dakota and Virginia, part performance of an obligation, either before or after a breach thereof, when expressly accepted in satisfaction by the creditor in writing or rendered in pursuance of an agreement in writing for that purpose, though without any new consideration, extinguishes the obligation. In Colorado, accord and satisfaction may not be applied to liquidated bonding obligations. In Mississippi, Ohio, South Carolina and Virginia, a creditor may settle or compromise with a joint debtor without releasing the co-debtors for the amount remaining due and unpaid. Accord and satisfaction must be specially pleaded in Alabama, California, Colorado, Connecticut, the District of Columbia, Indiana, Iowa, Kansas, Kentucky, Maryland, Massachusetts, Mississippi, Nevada, New Jersey, New York, Oklahoma, Pennsylvania, South Dakota, Tennessee, Texas and Vermont.[47]

The principal effect of a valid compromise is that it impedes further litigation about doubtful and uncertain causes. It has the force of a *res iudicata*.[48] As such it may be proposed as an effective per-

[46] Bouvier, *Law Dictionary*, s.v. "Accord and Satisfaction."

[47] These facts may be found along with additional information on this subject under the headings of the various states under the title "Accord and Satisfaction" in the *Martindale-Hubbell Law Directory* (74. annual ed., 2 vols., Summit, N. J.: Martindale-Hubbell, Inc., 1943), II. There is no pagination indicated in this work.

[48] C. 1, X, *de transactionibus*, I, 36; Wernz, *Ius Decretalium*, V, n. 46; Noval, *De Iudiciis*, n. 721; Coronata, *Institutiones*, n. 1446.

emptory exception.[49] It will therefore impede further introduction of the same cause.[50]

The exception is to be made known by the judge *ex officio,* for a matter that has been settled previously should not be made the object of a trial.[51] The *exceptio transactionis* will not be valid, however, unless as in the case of the exception of *res iudicata,* (1) the object of the suit and the object of the transaction be the same; (2) the cause of the transaction and the cause of the suit be identical; and (3) the same condition of persons concur.[52] If not all three of these conditions are present, the exception will not be admissible.[53]

Third parties may not use the *exceptio transactionis,* for a contract affects only those who are parties to the contract.[54] On the same basis this exception may not be proposed against a third party.

The exception should be placed as soon as possible in order to avoid a useless procedure. Since it is of the *litis finitae* category, the Code requires that it be placed and proved before the joinder of issue.[55] As such, it impedes the joinder of issue.[56]

It seems that the matter of this exception can be settled by means of a decree, for the question should be decided easily without extensive proofs and many witnesses.[57] A copy of the contract determining the compromise, or the testimony of the witnesses attesting to it, should be sufficient to settle this exception, unless there be difficulty in deciding the identity of the compromise with the cause that is pleaded.

[49] Canon 1629, § 1.

[50] Canon 1904, § 2.

[51] Canon 1742, § 1. Cf. Roberti, *De Processibus,* II, n. 509; Coronata, *Institutiones,* n. 1425.

[52] Schmalzgrueber, lib. II, tit. XXV, n. 47; Bouix, *De Iudiciis Ecclesiasticis,* II, 177; Coronata, *Institutiones,* III, n. 1425; Roberti, *De Processibus,* II, n. 513.

[53] Coronata, *Institutiones,* III, n. 1425.

[54] C. 25, X, *de sententia et re iudicata,* II, 27; Schmalzgrueber, lib. II, tit. XXVII, n. 81.

[55] Canon 1629.

[56] Cc. 1, 2, *de litis contestatione,* II, 3, in VI°; Schmalzgrueber, lib. II, tit. XXV, n. 23; Wernz, *Ius Decretalium,* V, n. 419.

[57] Muñiz, *Procedimientos Eclesiásticos,* III, n. 179; Wernz-Vidal, *Ius Canonicum,* VI, n. 548; Coronata, *Institutiones,* III, n. 1372.

Article 3. Arbitration

Another means of avoiding trial is to commit the settlement of the dispute to one or more persons who as arbiters will decide the question according to the rules of law, or as arbitrators will settle it according to the rules of equity.[58]

The same laws which hold in the case of valid compromise are applied to arbitration.[59]

Since arbitration differs from compromise only in the manner of settling the cause, it will also hold as a valid peremptory exception with the effect of a *res iudicata.* As a result the cause will be considered definitely adjudicated, and the introduction of the same cause in court will be impeded.[60]

If the evidence indicates that the matter in question has been settled by arbitration, the judge should advert to it *ex officio* and quash the suit in order to avoid unnecessary litigation.[61] If the defendant realizes that he has the use of such an exception he should place it before the joinder of issue, since this exception is of the *litis finitae* category and will impede the joinder of issue.[62]

Since settlement by arbitration partakes of the aspects of a contract,[63] only those who are parties to the instrument may make use of it. Hence third parties are excluded.[64]

In order that the exception may be valid, the circumstances of the arbitration and the circumstances of the suit, viz., the object, cause and condition of persons, must be identical.[65]

The civil law is also to be considered in the application of the principles of arbitration.[66] In American Civil Law the canonical

[58] Canon 1929.

[59] Canons 1930; 1926; 1927.

[60] Canon 1904, § 2.

[61] Roberti, *De Processibus,* II, n. 509; Coronata, *Institutiones,* n. 1425.

[62] Canon 1629; cc. 1, 2, *de litis contestatione,* II, 3, in VI°; Schmalzgrueber, lib. II, tit. XXV, n. 23; Reiffenstuel, lib. II, tit. XXV, n. 50; Wernz, *Ius Decretalium,* V, n. 419.

[63] Canons 1930; 1926; 1927.

[64] Schmalzgrueber, lib. II, tit. XXVII, n. 81.

[65] Schmalzgrueber, lib. II, tit. XXV, n. 47; Bouix, *De Iudiciis Ecclesiasticis,* II, 177; Coronata, *Institutiones,* n. 1425; Roberti, *De Processibus,* n. 513.

[66] Canons 1930; 1926.

term is represented by the legal terminology of *arbitration and award.*[67]

ARTICLE 4. DECISORY OATH

A decisory oath, by which a party swears to the truth of the facts alleged after being challenged to take such an oath by his adversary, has the effect of deciding the issue; it has the force of a *res iudicata;* it is considered the same as a valid compromise.[68]

The oath is *judicial* if it is made during the course of the trial, *extrajudicial* if it takes place outside the trial.[69] The approval of the judge is necessary for employing the judicial decisory oath.[70] He determines whether or not the conditions necessary for the use of the oath are present. If he decides that the use of the oath is valid, he will issue a decree indicating this. He will also indicate the subject matter of the oath.[71]

The judge should also consider the character of both parties

[67] The process is described as "the investigation and determination of a matter or matters of difference between contending parties, by one or more unofficial persons, chosen by the parties, and called arbitrators or referees. It usually takes place in pursuance of an agreement (commonly in writing) between the parties, termed a submission; and the determination of the arbitrators or referees is called an award; but a parol submission is good as common law. A submission to arbitration made pending an action thereon, operates as a discontinuance of the suit; 76 Cal. 378; and it is a bar to any future action thereon; 129, Ind. 185. If the submission is not made under an order of court, the award cannot be made a judgment of the court unless it be by consent; 97 N.C. 39. Any matter may be determined by arbitration which the parties may adjust by agreement, or which may be the subject of a suit at law. Crimes, however, and perhaps actions on penal statutes by common informers, cannot be made the subject of adjustment and composition by arbitration. Everyone is so far, and only so far, bound by the award as he would be by an agreement of the same kind made directly by him. For example, the submission of a minor is not void, but voidable." Cf. Bouvier, *Law Dictionary,* s.v. "*Arbitration and Award.*"

[68] Canon 1834. Cf. Wernz, *Ius Decretalium,* V, n. 645; Coronata, *Institutiones,* n. 1466; Noval, *De Iudiciis,* n. 573; Roberti, *De Processibus,* n. 389.

[69] Roberti, *De Processibus,* n. 389.

[70] Canon 1834, § 1; Coronata, *Institutiones,* n. 1366.

[71] Moriarty, *Oaths in Ecclesiastical Courts,* p. 86.

before permitting the oath, because it is possible that the person who is challenged to take the oath may in turn challenge the other party to take it. As a result, it would not be possible for him to foretell who will take the oath eventually.[72] He should not, for instance, allow the oath if one of the parties has been guilty of perjury.[73]

Although the judge may suggest that the oath be employed, the parties are not bound to accede to this suggestion. On the other hand, if the judge denies the parties the use of the oath, there is basis for an appeal.[74]

Certain conditions are required for the valid use of the decisory oath: (1) It must concern a matter in which cession and compromise are admitted, and which is not of considerably great importance or value to the litigants.[75] Noval identifies cession with donation.[76] According to this interpretation, prelates and rectors would be allowed the use of the decisory oath only when the disputed amount is in accordance with the amount permitted to be given as donations by local customs unless a just cause such as charity, reward or piety should be present, warranting a larger sum; [77] religious would be denied the use of the oath concerning matters or amounts which are limited by the superior's permission or local constitutions.[78] If the object of the dispute is of considerably great importance there will be danger of perjury.[79] The judge can determine the value of the matter involved according to the civil law.[80]

[72] Wernz-Vidal, *Ius Canonicum,* VI, n. 542.

[73] Moriarty, *op. cit.,* pp. 90, 91.

[74] Coronata, *Institutiones,* n. 1367; Moriarty, *op. cit.,* p. 86.

[75] Canon 1835, 1°. The civil law is also to be followed as a guiding norm in the admission of the oath because of its aspects as a compromise (canon 1926). The judge should not allow the oath if, e.g., the civil law has excluded the object in question from compromise or its value is more than that allowed by the civil law for legitimate compromise. Cf. Noval, *De Iudiciis,* n. 573; Moriarty, *op. cit.,* p. 91.

[76] *De Iudiciis,* n. 573.

[77] Canon 1535.

[78] Canon 537. Cf. Moriarty, *op. cit.,* p. 86.

[79] Augustine, *Commentary,* VIII, 280.

[80] Coronata, *Institutiones,* n. 1367; Noval, *De Iudiciis,* n. 573; Roberti, *De Processibus,* n. 390.

(2) The person who tenders or takes the oath must be capable of ceding his right or of making a private settlement.[81] In order to employ the agency of cession or of compromise, a person must possess the faculty to dispose of his rights. One who is excluded by law from such action is therefore also excluded from tendering or taking the decisory oath. The following, then, are excluded: (a) infants, the insane and feeble minded persons; (b) those not permitted to stand in trial; (c) religious without the consent of their superiors; (d) procurators without a special mandate.[82]

Representatives of moral persons do not need any further qualification for the use of the oath if they have entered the trial legitimately.[83] However, a just cause must be present and the solemnities for alienation must be observed.[84]

(3) If a person has given full proof, he cannot be challenged to take the oath.[85] The decisory oath is usually resorted to when the available evidence is not sufficient for the proof of the facts alleged. Otherwise there would not be any necessity for the oath. It is an extraordinary means of arriving at the truth.[86]

Moriarty [87] summarizes the "principles of the decisory oath in its relation to the presentation of proof:

1. The decisory oath cannot be tendered to a party who has fully proved his case.[88]

2. The decisory oath can be employed when both parties furnish equal proof.[89]

3. The decisory oath can be tendered *to* a party who has furnished no proof or less than full proof.[90]

[81] Canon 1835, 2°, 3°.

[82] Canons 1646-1654; 1662; Lega, *De Iudiciis Ecclesiasticis,* I, n. 9; Moriarty, *op. cit.,* p. 91.

[83] Roberti, *De Processibus,* n. 390; Wernz-Vidal, *Ius Canonicum,* VI, n. 544.

[84] Wernz-Vidal, *Ius Canonicum,* VI, n. 666.

[85] Canon 1836, 3°.

[86] Roberti, *De Processibus,* II, n. 390.

[87] *Op. cit.,* p. 92.

[88] Canon 1835, 3°.

[89] Coronata, *Institutiones,* n. 1367.

[90] Wernz-Vidal, *Ius Canonicum,* VI, n. 542.

4. The decisory oath can be tendered *by* a party who has furnished no proof or less than full proof." [91]

(4) The matter of the oath must concern a fact which is personal to the oath-taker or known by him.[92] The oath would be especially expedient when the fact would be known only to the oath-taker.[93]

Knowledge of the fact may have been attained either directly or indirectly, however.[94] If the one who takes the oath has obtained his knowledge of the matter directly, the oath is designated *de scientia;* if he has obtained it indirectly, it is termed *de credulitate.*[95]

The challenge to take the oath may be recalled by the one who suggested it as long as the oath has not been taken as yet. It may also be accepted or rejected, given or not given by the opponent, and the latter may even reverse the order and challenge his adversary to take it even after he himself has been challenged.[96]

After the oath has been taken, the same effects are obtained as are had in the case of a valid cession or compromise.[97] The issue is definitely decided to the extent that there is no appeal.[98] The decision has the force of a *res iudicata* with all its implications.[99] Because of its similarity to a compromise, the decisory oath will not be admitted in causes in which a compromise is not admitted.[100]

If the oath is refused after the challenge has been made, the judge will weigh the refusal: whether it is just or whether perhaps it constitutes a confession of guilt.[101] If the judge decides that the refusal constitutes a confession the trial will be concluded in favor of the other party. If the causes for refusing the oath are valid the trial will proceed on its own merits.

[91] Roberti, *De Processibus,* II, n. 390.

[92] Canon 1835, 4°. Cf. Moriarty, *op. cit.,* p. 93.

[93] *Regulae servandae in iudiciis apud S.R. Rotae Tribunal,* 4 aug. 1910, n. 150—*AAS,* II (1910), 829.

[94] Roberti, *De Processibus,* n. 390.

[95] Canon 1789, 2°.

[96] Canon 1836, § 1.

[97] Canon 1836, § 2.

[98] Canon 1880, 5°; Lega, *De Iudiciis Ecclesiasticis,* I, nn. 465, 471.

[99] Roberti, *De Processibus,* n. 392; Wernz-Vidal, *Ius Canonicum,* VI, n. 543.

[100] Canon 1927, § 1.

[101] Canons 1836, § 3; 1835; 1927, § 1.

The principal effect of the decisory oath with regard to the institute of exceptions is that if the defendant has taken the oath, or if the plaintiff has refused to take the oath at the instance of the defendant or the judge, the *exceptio iuratoria* may be claimed by the defendant in any subsequent action brought against him by the plaintiff.[102] The exception will quash the suit if the object, cause and condition of persons of both the oath and the trial are identical.[103]

The exception, being of the *litis finitae* type, should be placed and proved before the joinder of issue, since the issue cannot be joined if it is proved that the exception exists.[104] The exception need not necessarily be placed by the parties alone; the judge should advert to it *ex officio* if he sees that it exists. The common good requires that useless procedure should be avoided.[105]

Third parties may not make use of this exception because it partakes of the nature of a contract.[106] For the same reason it may not be employed against a third party.

It should be possible to settle this exception by a mere decree, for the acts of the case in which the oath was taken will provide the necessary evidence.

Article 5. Nullity of the Sentence

In Roman Law the plaint of nullity as a means of attacking a sentence was unknown. However, a declaration of nullity could be obtained to prevent the execution of the sentence.[107] The sentence was null if it was pronounced by an incompetent judge, if it was contrary to a positive law or to a judgment already given, if it decreed

[102] Schmalzgrueber, lib. II, tit. XXIV, n. 20; Wernz, *Ius Decretalium,* V, n. 645; Coronata, *Institutiones,* n. 1366.

[103] Schmalzgrueber, lib. II, tit. XXV, n. 47; Bouix, *De Iudiciis Ecclesiasticis,* II, 177; Coronata, *Institutiones,* n. 1425; Roberti, *De Processibus,* n. 513.

[104] Canon 1629; cc. 1, 2, *de litis contestatione,* II, 3, in VI°; Schmalzgrueber, lib. II, tit. XXV, n. 23; Reiffenstuel, lib. II, tit. XXV, n. 50; Wernz, *Ius Decretalium,* V, n. 419.

[105] Canon 1742, § 1; Roberti, *De Processibus,* n. 509; Coronata, *Institutiones,* n. 1425.

[106] Schmalzgrueber, lib. II, tit. XXVII, n. 81.

[107] D. (49.1) 19; C. (1.14) 15.

what was impossible of execution, if the basic rules of procedure were not observed, or if one of the parties lacked the capacity of bringing suit.[108]

Under the ancient canonical discipline there seems to be no evidence of a remedy against the nullity of a sentence outside of an appeal.[109]

In the middle ages the exception of nullity was gradually introduced,[110] and finally in the thirteenth century, at the time of Innocent III, the action of nullity came into being.[111] At first the plaint of nullity was made before the judge who gave the sentence,[112] but as time went on it became customary to have the plaint of nullity invariably made to the judge of appeal.[113] The Code has restored the plaint of nullity as an institute entirely distinct from the appeal, although in some cases it may accompany the appeal.[114]

The plaint of nullity is a remedy against the judicial sentence by which it is contended that the sentence is null, for the reason that it labors under a substantial defect.[115] The plaint of nullity differs intrinsically from the appeal in that it is interposed because of a defect extrinsic to the sentence, in other words, a defect of form, while, on the contrary, the appeal is made because of an intrinsic defect in the sentence, in so far as the sentence is unjust, i.e., does not conform to the rights of the parties.[116] The plaint of nullity is

[108] C. (50.1); (64.1).

[109] Cf. c. 1, X, *de sententia et re iudicata,* II, 27.

[110] Cf. c. 4, X, *de procuratoribus,* I, 38.

[111] Roberti, *De Processibus,* n. 486.

[112] Cf. c. 4, X, *de procuratoribus,* I, 38.

[113] Reiffenstuel, lib. II, tit. XXVIII, n. 31; Bouix, *De Iudiciis,* II, 410.

[114] Canons 1880, 3°; 1892-1897.

[115] Coronata, *Institutiones,* n. 1417.

[116] Wernz-Vidal, *Ius Canonicum,* VI, n. 614; Coronata, *loc. cit.* Lega-Bartoccetti (*Commentarius,* II, 1015) place the substantial difference between the plaint of nullity and the appeal in that the former is presented before the same judge who issued the sentence, while the latter is made to a higher judge. This does not seem correct, since for many centuries before the Code the plaint of nullity was made to a higher tribunal, and also since even under the Code canon 1895 permits the plaint of nullity to accompany the appeal in certain cases. Besides the plaint of nullity as an exception may be made before any tribunal.

likewise distinguished from ***restitutio in integrum,***[117] an extraordinary remedy which natural equity prompts the lawgiver to provide in cases in which all other remedies (i.e., the plaint of nullity, the appeal, court actions to rescind acts performed through force and fear) are out of the question.[118]

A sentence which is null must be distinguished from a sentence which does not exist. A sentence is said not to exist when it does not proceed from judicial authority, or if it does not have the semblance of a sentence, e.g., if the sentence is issued by one who is not a judge, or if only the private conclusions of the judges are presented. In these cases it is enough to examine the purported sentence to discern that it is not a true sentence. No special action is required to attack its validity.[119]

A sentence which is null, on the other hand, is one which is legitimately issued by the judge and bears the semblance of a true sentence, but so labors under a defect that it cannot be upheld.[120]

The plaint of nullity can be made either as an action or as an exception.[121] It is as an exception that it is here considered. The plaint of nullity can be made by way of a perpetual exception, which amounts to a peremptory exception when the judge is opposed and estopped in the execution of the sentence, or the victorious party is estopped in vindicating a sentence pronounced in his favor.[122]

The nullity of a sentence may be remediable or irremediable. Lega-Bartoccetti believe that the basis of this distinction is to be found in the fact that the former is based upon the private advantage of the parties, and so may be waived by the parties, either expressly, or tacitly (by allowing the time limit to elapse), while, on

[117] Cf. canons 1687-1689; 1905-1907.

[118] Reiffenstuel, lib. I, tit. XLI, n. 3; Feeney, *Restitutio in Integrum,* pp. 1-2, 49-50. Roberti (*De Processibus,* II, n. 486) notes that before the Code the Rota frequently did not make a clear-cut distinction between the cases which called for the plaint of nullity and those in which the *restitutio in integrum* was demanded.

[119] Roberti, *De Processibus,* n. 487.

[120] Roberti, *loc. cit.*

[121] Canons 1893; 1667.

[122] Lega-Bartoccetti, *Commentarius,* II, 1023; Augustine, *Commentary,* VII, 330; Coronata, *Institutiones,* n. 1417.

the other hand, irremediable nullities have been determined for the public good, and so cannot be waived by private individuals.[123] Roberti,[124] on the other hand, places the distinction only in the difference of time after which, with respect to the gravity of the cases, the action of nullity is concluded. This view seems to disregard completely the plaint of nullity as an exception.

Although the point is not expressly mentioned by any of the authors, it seems clear that the plaint of nullity as an exception can be used only in connection with irremediable nullities, and does not apply to remediable nullities.[125] This view is based upon the fact that canon 1893, in stating that the plaint of nullity can be proposed either as an exception or as an action, refers specifically to the irremediable nullities of canon 1892. The wording of the canon and its place between canons 1892 and 1894 evidently indicates that it refers to the former, and not to the latter. In the second place, canon 1895 explicitly places time limits upon the use of the plaint of nullity with regard to the remediable nullities of canon 1894. Since the exception of canon 1893 is perpetual,[126] it, therefore, cannot have a place with regard to the remediable nullities of canon 1894, which are sanated if the plaint of nullity is neither introduced nor the sentence emendated within the time stipulated in law.[127] For

[123] Lega-Bartoccetti, *Commentarius,* II, 1015; this view is also accepted by Vermeersch-Creusen (*Epitome,* II, n. 241) and Wernz-Vidal (*Ius Canonicum,* VI, n. 614).

[124] *De Processibus,* n. 488.

[125] The fact that the plaint of nullity as an exception has a place only with regard to irremediable nullities is implied by the various authors who mention it as an exception only when discussing irremediable nullities, although Blat (*Commentarium Textus Codicis Iuris Canonici, Liber IV, De Processibus,* n. 428), in discussing who may present the plaint of nullity under canon 1897, uses words which could bear the implication that a remediable nullity may be attacked by the plaint of nullity as an exception.

[126] "Nullitas de qua in can. 1892 proponi potest per modum exceptionis in perpetuum . . . "—Canon 1893. In any event an exception is perpetual by its very nature.—Roberti, *De Processibus,* I, n. 275; Canon 1667: " . . . exceptione, quae semper competit, et est suapte natura perpetua." Cf. also canon 1698, § 2.

[127] S. C. de Sacr., instr. 15 aug. 1936, art. 211, § 3—*AAS,* XXVIII (1936), 313-361, in particular pp. 354-355.

this reason this treatise will consider only the nullity of a sentence which is irremediable.

A sentence is invalid in consequence of irremediable nullity in the following cases: (1) when it is issued by a tribunal which is absolutely incompetent, or one that has not the requisite number of judges demanded by canon 1576, § 1; (2) when it has been pronounced in the case of parties, one of whom at least has not the legal right to bring suit in an ecclesiastical tribunal; (3) when one has prosecuted a case in another person's name without the lawful mandate to do so.[128]

(1) No tribunal is competent to judge the Holy See.[129] In addition, a diocesan tribunal would be absolutely incompetent to judge cases involving the persons mentioned in canon 1557, some of which are reserved to the Roman Pontiff, others to the tribunals of the Holy See. Further, a tribunal which has judged a case in one instance is absolutely incompetent to judge the same case in another instance.[130]

The sentence is irremediably null if it has been rendered by a tribunal having a number of judges less than that prescribed by law. Three judges are required by law for cases involving the bond of ordination or matrimony, and for some criminal cases of removal from office or excommunication. Five judges are required for the tribunal which pronounces sentence in criminal cases of deposition and degradation.[131] What if a case were committed not to three or five but to four or six judges? Certainly it is not essential to the nature of a tribunal that it should have an unequal number of judges.[132] However, the sanction of absolute nullity is clearly implied in the text of the law when it is prescribed that the number of

[128] Canon 1892.

[129] Canon 1556.

[130] Canon 1571.

[131] Canon 1576, § 1. The violation of the rules of canons 1572, § 2, 1576, § 2, and 1596 does not involve irremediable nullity.—Roberti, *De Processibus*, n. 490; Muñiz, *Procedimientos Eclesiásticos*, III, 425; Coronata, *Institutiones*, n. 1418.

[132] In its ancient constitution the Rota provided for an equal number of judges.—Lega-Bartoccetti, *Commentarius*, II, 1018.

judges should be legitimate, that is, as ordained by law. Moreover, this prescription of law pertains to the public law of the Church which may not be changed by private authority.[133]

When a sentence is declared null because of the absolute incompetence of the tribunal, all the acts of the case and of the process are null. When the sentence is declared null because of the lack of the legitimate number of judges, only those acts are null which require the intervention of the whole tribunal.[134]

(2) The sentence is irremediably null when it has been pronounced on parties one of whom was not entitled to bring suit in an ecclesiastical court. Non-Catholics, whether baptized or not, may not be plaintiffs in matrimonial causes.[135] Likewise the spouses who are responsible for the impediment may not seek a judicial declaration of the nullity of their marriage.[136] Ordination may be judicially impugned only by the cleric or the Ordinary whose subject he is or in whose diocese he was ordained.[137] Only the cleric himself can seek a declaration of nullity of the obligations imposed by ordination.[138] Those who are under a condemnatory or declaratory sentence of excommunication, whether as *vitandi* or *tolerati*, are excluded from ecclesiastical trials; [139] although they are allowed to act as plaintiffs if they wish to impugn the justice or legitimacy of the sentence of excommunication, and they may act through a procurator to ward off spiritual injury.[140]

(3) A sentence is irremediably null if a person prosecutes a case in the name of another without the lawful mandate to do so.

133 Lega-Bartoccetti, *loc. cit.*

134 Muñiz, *Procedimientos Eclesiásticos,* III, 502; Coronata, *Institutiones,* n. 1418; Wernz-Vidal, *Ius Canonicum,* VI, n. 621.

135 S. C. S. Officii, 27 ian. 1928—*AAS,* XX (1928), 75. From this Roberti (*De Processibus,* II, n. 490) makes the deduction that non-Catholics may not be plaintiffs in any ecclesiastical trial, stating that although the declaration of the Holy Office refers to matrimonial causes the principle is general.

136 Canon 1971, § 1, 1°.

137 Canon 1994, § 1.

138 Canon 1994, § 2.

139 Canon 1628, § 3.

140 Canon 1654.

A special mandate in writing to undertake litigation is required.[141] Hence in cases undertaken by procurators without the proper authorization, the sentence is irremediably null.[142]

There is no doubt that besides the cases enumerated in canons 1892 and 1894 the sentence can be affected by many other defects. The question is whether a plaint of nullity can be made in regard to such defects, or whether the sentence so vitiated is rescissible. This is a matter of practical importance in deciding whether the sentence is to be attacked by the plaint of nullity or by the use of *restitutio in integrum* when there are violations of the laws of procedure. If the enumeration of the above-mentioned canons is all inclusive, then *restitutio in integrum* should be used.[143] If it is not all-inclusive, then the plaint of nullity may be applied.

Roberti holds that the list of causes entailing the nullity of a sentence given in canons 1892 and 1894 is not all-inclusive; [144] that there are other nullities for which the sentence may be attacked by a plaint of nullity. D'Angelo [145] and others [146] maintain that the

[141] Canon 1892, 1°; canon 1659, § 1; S. C. de Sacr., instr. 15 aug. 1936, art. 49—*AAS,* XXVIII (1936), 324.

[142] Canons 1892, 1°; 1651; S. C. de Sacr., instr. 15 aug. 1936, art. 78—*AAS,* XXVIII (1936), 330.

[143] Canon 1905, § 2, 4°, provides for the use of *restitutio in integrum* against an evidently unjust sentence in the following case: "Legis praescriptum evidenter neglectum fuerit."

[144] *De Processibus,* nn. 491-494; "Circa limites querelae nullitatis et restitutionis in integrum,"—*Apollinaris,* I (1928), 476-483. This view is also held by the following: Lemieux, *The Sentence in Ecclesiastical Procedure,* pp. 99, 102; Hanssen, "De Sanatione nullitatis in processu canonico,"—*Apollinaris,* XII (1939), 238-249.

[145] "Un caso di 'restitutio in integrum' nella vigente disciplina canonica,"—*Ephemerides Theologicae Lovanienses,* III (1926), 355-360; "De Restitutione in Integrum iuxta canonem 1905, § 2, 4°,"—*Periodica,* XVIII (1929), 37*-62*.

[146] Muñiz, *Procedimientos Eclesiásticos,* III, n. 505; Wernz-Vidal, *Ius Canonicum,* VI, n. 623; Feeney, *Restitutio in Integrum,* pp. 110-130. Coronata (*Institutiones,* III, n. 1418) holds that in cases of nullity outside those enumerated in canons 1892 and 1894 the Code does not concede the plaint of nullity, but that in such cases the sentence which is null is to be attacked either through appeal or by *restitutio in integrum.* Lega-Bartoccetti (*Commentarius,* II, 1025-1026) consider the enumeration in canon 1892 all-inclusive, but not the listing in canon 1894.

use of the plaint of nullity is strictly limited to the cases listed in canons 1892 and 1894.

In favor of Roberti's opinion may be adduced the fact that canon 1679 allows an action for the declaration of the nullity of any act. Roberti places great stress on the words of canon 1680, § 2, which declares that the nullity of an act does not imply the nullity of a preceding or succeeding act upon which it does not depend. From this he deduces the existence of a derived nullity, namely that an act is null because of the nullity of another act in the process upon which it depends.[147] In the procedural law of the Code there are many formalities whose omission results in the nullity of the acts of the trial. For instance, the acts of the process which are not signed by the notary are declared null by canon 1585, § 1; according to canon 1587, § 1, in a case wherein the citation or at least the presence of the defender of the bond or of the promoter of justice is required, the acts are null if these officials are not cited or at least present. The sentence depends upon the acts of the case.[148] If the process is invalid then the sentence at the conclusion of such a process is null as the result of a derived nullity. It is not likely that the sentence is to be excepted from this general rule.[149] Violations of the natural law as well as of the positive law will nullify a sentence. Both the Signatura and the Rota have asserted this since the promulgation of the Code.[150]

According to this view, any sentence which is null for the reason that it is the conclusion of an invalid sentence is to be attacked by a plaint of nullity, even though the nullity is not one of those listed in canons 1892 and 1894. Although most of the violations of procedural law will be remediable and therefore possible of sanation,[151] some will subject the sentence to irremediable nullity, either because they concern the public good, such as the neglect of the re-

[147] Roberti, *De Processibus,* nn. 241; 487; 492.

[148] Canon 1869, § 2, states that the judge should obtain the moral certainty, required in pronouncing sentence, from the acts and proofs of the case.

[149] Roberti, *De Processibus,* n. 492.

[150] Signatura, *De Manila,* 6 apr. 1920—*AAS,* XII (1920), 256; *Paderbornen.,* 10 mart. 1919—*AAS,* XI (1919), 296-297.

[151] E.g., those mentioned in canons 1585, § 1; 1740, § 2; 1637; 1855.

quirements that the defender of the bond should be cited or at least present in causes concerning the bond of ordination or matrimony; [152] or because the provision of the positive law is based upon the dictates of the natural law, e.g., the denial of a legitimate defense.[153] If Roberti's opinion is followed, the plaint of nullity as an exception could be used in such cases.[154]

The main argument for the view that the listing of the nullities in canons 1892 and 1894 is all-inclusive is taken from a comparison of the Code with the preparatory *Schemata* drawn up before the adoption of the Code. In the *Schema* of 1914 the plaint of nullity was provided for in cases wherein the process was vitiated by any defect of nullity, and a list of nullities was given which was clearly demonstrative.[155] Five of the preparatory *Schemata* listed as a reason for the nullity of the sentence the fact that it was the conclusion of an invalid process as a result of the violation of procedural law in the case.[156] The Code omits mention of the nullity of the sentence resulting from the nullity of the process.[157] As a further argument in favor of D'Angelo's opinion is the desire which the episcopate conveyed to the preparatory commission that the number of nullities be reduced in number.[158]

Since the controversy as to whether the listing of nullities in canons 1892 and 1894 is or is not all-inclusive still awaits an official decision, the while eminent authors defend each side with solid arguments a doubt of law exists.[159] Parties who wish to obtain legal redress against the damage inflicted by the violation of the procedural laws not mentioned in canons 1392 and 1894, should petition

[152] Canons 1586; 1587, § 1; 1967; 1996.

[153] Canon 1861, § 2.

[154] Cf. *supra*, pp. 108-109.

[155] *Codicis Iuris Canonici Schemata, Liber IV, De Processibus, I, De Iudiciis in Genere* (digessit F. Roberti, Civitate Vaticana: Typis Polyglottis Vaticanis, 1940), 437.

[156] *Codicis Iuris Canonici Schemata, Liber IV, De Processibus*, I, 435-437.

[157] Canons 1892, 1894.

[158] Roberti, "Codici iuris canonici Schemata de processibus,"—*Acta Congressus Iuridici Internationalis 1934,* IV, 33.

[159] Feeney, *Restitutio in Integrum*, p. 129; Król, *The Defendant in Contentious Trials*, p. 180.

for the application of the extraordinary remedy of ***restitutio in integrum***, with the added request that if this remedy does not apply to the case, a declaration of nullity should be issued against the sentence. Until such time when the jurisprudence of the Roman Tribunals by clear and repeated decisions solves the question, or when an authentic interpretation is given by the Pontifical Commission for the Interpretation of the Code, the judge is free to adopt either of the two conflicting opinions.[160]

The plaint of nullity may be brought not only by the parties who think themselves aggrieved, but also by the promoter of justice or the defender of the bond, when they have taken part in the trial.[161] The victor has also the right to bring the plea of nullity against the sentence, because in the event that such a sentence will be harmful to him for the reason that it cannot be lawfully executed.[162] The procurator may propose the plaint of nullity unless the mandate authorizing him to represent the parties has been expressly or tacitly revoked.[163]

Even the judge may *ex officio* retract an invalid sentence issued by him and correct it within the terms prescribed by law.[164] That the judge can take this course in criminal trials, and in those which concern the public good of the Church or the salvation of souls, is evident.[165] But he can also take cognizance of the nullity of a sentence involving private interests only, because the sentence itself, being so essential to the proper administration of justice, always concerns the public good. Besides, natural justice demands that one retract

[160] Cf. Roberti, *De Processibus*, II, n. 523, in fine.

[161] Canon 1897, § 1.

[162] Roberti, *De Processibus*, II, n. 498; Coronata, *Institutiones*, n. 1420.

[163] Wernz-Vidal, *Ius Canonicum*, VI, n. 617; Coronata, *loc. cit.*; Muñiz, *Procedimientos Eclesiásticos*, III, 479; Doheny, *Canonical Procedure in Matrimonial Cases*, p. 347. Cf. S. C. de Sacr., instr. 15 aug. 1936, art. 44, § 2, which says: "Procuratoris est, partem repraesentare, libellos aut *recursus cuiuscumque generis* tribunali exhibere."—*AAS*, XXVIII (1936), 323. Roberti (*op. cit.*, n. 500) states that the procurator needs a new mandate in order to present the plea of nullity, at least if the process is to be renewed *ex integro*.

[164] Canon 1897, § 2.

[165] Canon 1618.

those acts of his which are injurious to others, as long as it is in his power.[166]

The person responsible for the nullity of a sentence is bound to pay for any damages which it causes.[167]

The plaint of nullity as an exception, since it is perpetual, can be brought before any tribunal.[168] The proviso that the plaint of nullity in cases of irremediable nullity may be presented only before the judge who issued the sentence is laid down by canon 1893 for actions but not for exceptions.[169]

If the party making the plea of nullity as an exception fears that the tribunal which judged the case is prejudiced, but prefers to make his plea in the same instance, he may avail himself of the provision of canon 1896 and demand that another judge or other judges be substituted in the same tribunal.[170]

A plaint of nullity against a sentence of the Rota is to be made to the Apostolic Signatura.[171] When a plaint of nullity against a Rota decision is presented to the Signatura, this tribunal is to judge only whether the Rotal sentence is null or not. After the Signatura has rendered judgment on this point, the case must be sent back to the Rota, unless the Holy Father provides otherwise.[172]

166 Roberti, *De Processibus*, n. 498; Coronata, *Institutiones*, n. 1420; Wernz-Vidal, *Ius Canonicum*, VI, n. 620. Lega-Bartoccetti (*Commentarius*, II, 1032), on the contrary, state that the provisions of canon 1897, § 2, do not apply to the judge in purely contentious causes, namely in those which involve private interests only.

167 Roberti, *De Processibus*, II, n. 488. Cf. canon 1625, §§ 1, 3.

168 Canon 1667. Cf. Reiffenstuel, lib. II, tit. XXVI, n. 66; Coronata, *Institutiones*, n. 1419; Vermeersch-Creusen, *Epitome*, III, n. 242; Doheny, *Canonical Procedure in Matrimonial Cases*, p. 346.

169 Lega-Bartoccetti (*Commentarius*, II, 1029), contrary to other canonists, hold that the plaint of nullity as an action may be joined with the appeal not only with regard to sentences null in consequence of a remediable nullity, but also when the sentence is irremediably null. Cf. canon 1895.

170 Cf. S. C. de Sacr., instr. 15 aug. 1936, art. 211, § 4—*AAS*, XXVIII (1936), 355.

171 Canon 1603, § 1, 3°.

172 Canon 1604, § 3.

Roberti[173] and Vermeersch-Creusen[174] take the view that the mandate of a judge delegated for one case is not completed[175] when he renders a sentence which is null; he is therefore competent to accept the plaint of nullity.[176] Two reasons are given for this view: (1) The Code in canons 1893 and 1895 does not distinguish between ordinary judges and delegated judges. (2) This is confirmed by analogy with canon 59, § 1, by virtue of which, if the executor makes any mistake in the execution of rescripts, he has the right to repeat the execution. Before the Code the faculty of recognizing the plaint of nullity was given to judges delegated *ad universitatem causarum,* not to those delegated for certain cases. When the latter rendered sentence their office ceased.[177] Noval and others hold that this is still the case under the Code.[178]

When the plaint of nullity is proposed, whether as an action or as an exception, the general norms governing trials are to be followed.[179] The libellus must list the reasons for attacking the sentence, i.e., the cause of the asserted nullity and the injury that would follow from such a sentence. The other party to the trial should be cited, as well as the defender of the bond, if he took part in the case. The promoter of justice should always be called to take part in the case when the plaint of nullity is presented, since the validity of a sentence concerns the public good.[180] The *litis contestatio* must also take place. After the process has proceeded in the ordinary manner, a sentence should be handed down. The sentence is subject to all the remedies of law.[181] Although judicial procedure is used in set-

[173] *De Processibus,* II, n. 497.

[174] *Epitome,* III, n. 242.

[175] Cf. canon 207, § 1.

[176] Coronata (*Institutiones,* n. 1419) seems to favor this opinion.

[177] This was based upon the regulation of Alexander III, in c. 9, X, *de officio et potestate iudicis delegati,* I, 29. Cf. Roberti, *De Processibus,* n. 497, and Wernz-Vidal, *Ius Canonicum,* VI, n. 622, footnote (13).

[178] Noval, *De Processibus,* n. 660; Lega-Bartoccetti, *Commentarius,* II, 1024, 1030; Wernz-Vidal, *Ius Canonicum,* VI, n. 618; Muñiz, *Procedimientos Eclesiásticos,* III, 479.

[179] Wernz-Vidal, *Ius Canonicum,* VI, n. 620; Roberti, *De Processibus,* n. 500.

[180] Wernz-Vidal, *loc. cit.*; Roberti, *loc. cit.*; Coronata, *Institutiones,* n. 1419.

[181] Roberti, *loc. cit.* Wernz-Vidal (*loc. cit.*) and Lega-Bartoccetti (*Com-

tling the plaint of nullity, the nature of the case calls for brevity and the reduction of delays, and the elimination of incidental questions.[182] Lega-Bartoccetti believe that the plaint of nullity may be presented as an incidental question, provided that it is made before the same tribunal which issued the sentence.[183] If the plaint of nullity is handled as an incidental question, the judge, in accordance with canon 1840, § 1, has the right to decide, either that the question be solved according to ordinary judicial procedure, or that a mere judicial decree be issued by him.[184]

When the plaint of nullity is presented, the judge must suspend execution of the sentence.[185]

mentarius, II, 1033; 1034) state that an appeal may be made against this sentence, but the latter (p. 1034, nota 1) claims that the plaint of nullity may not be invoked, to avoid a *processus in infinitum.*

182 Wernz-Vidal, *loc. cit.*

183 *Commentarius,* II, 1030, 1032-1033. The Code, in canon 1900, makes explicit provision for the use of the rules governing incidental causes in connection with the extraordinary remedy of *oppositio tertii,* but not for the plaint of nullity.

184 Cf. canons 1837-1841.

185 Although this is not stated in the Code, it seems logical that the provision enacted in this regard for the appeal in canon 1889, § 1, and for *restitutio in integrum* in canon 1907, § 1, should also apply to the plaint of nullity. Cf. Wernz-Vidal, *Ius Canonicum,* VI, n. 659, and Roberti, *De Processibus,* n. 547.

CHAPTER VI

SIMPLE PEREMPTORY EXCEPTIONS

THE effect of the simple peremptory exceptions will be determined in the rendering of the definitive sentence, for they will be judged accordingly as they affect the cause in question. They are to be considered after the joinder of issue and according to the manner of incidental questions.[1]

ARTICLE 1. FEAR

According to canon 1686 the exception of fear is granted to the defendant in case he is sued for the execution of an act or contract by a plaintiff who inflicted fear upon him.[2] The canonical doctrine on fear in the field of contracts has come largely from Roman Law sources. The terms *vis* and *metus* were taken from the Digest.[3] It was after the time of Alexander III (1159-1181) that these gradually supplanted the older canonical terms of *coactio modica* and *coactio violenta,* the latter of which had comprised both absolute and conditional force.[4] The definition of *vis* (absolute force) given by Paulus came into canonical doctrine—"Vis est maioris rei impetus, cui resisti non potest." [5] And Ulpian's definition of fear—"Metus est periculi causa mentis trepidatio" became standard in canonical terminology.[6]

The question of absolute physical force in regard to contracts offers no particular difficulty, since the natural law dictates that

[1] Canon 1629, § 2.

[2] "Si is qui metum intulit . . . , urgeat actus vel contractus executionem, parti laesae . . . competit exceptio metus. . . ."

[3] D. (4.2) 2.

[4] Cf. Kuttner, *Kanonistische Schuldlehre von Gratian bis auf die Dekretalen Gregors IX,* Studi e Testi, n. 64 (Città del Vaticano: Biblioteca Apostolica Vaticana, 1935), pp. 301-303, 308-309.

[5] D. (4.2) 2.

[6] D. (4.2) 2.

such force renders any attempted contract invalid. Such has always been the unanimous teaching of the canonists.[7] The question of conditional force, that is fear, is not so simple. By the time of Bernard of Parma (+1266) canonists were quite clear in maintaining that as a general rule acts performed because of fear were valid, but could be rescinded by the proper authority if the person suffering the fear was innocent of previous fault in the matter (*culpa praecedens*). There were some exceptions to this rule, namely those acts which were rendered null by grave, unjust fear. Such were considered marriage, the promise or gift of a dowry, the promise or gift of church property, a vow, the exercise of jurisdiction, or the authorization of a tutor.[8]

To understand clearly the requisites of the type of fear admitted as an exception in the court, it is necessary to review briefly the categories of fear as established by canonists in connection with the law of contracts. Fear is generally divided according to its cause into fear from within and fear from without. Fear from within (*ab intrinseco*) is all fear arising from some internal cause or from some external necessary cause. Fear from without (*ab extrinseco*) is that which is caused by a free created cause, a free human agent.[9]

Fear also differs according to the manner in which it is inflicted. Thus just fear and unjust fear are distinguished. Fear is unjust if the evil threatened is in some way unjust. This can be unjust either in itself or because of the concrete circumstances in which it is inflicted. The latter (*iniustus quoad modum*) is had when the one inflicting the fear has no competence in the matter, or even though

[7] Cf., e.g., Rufinus, *Summa Decretorum* (ed. Singer, Paderborn, 1902), ad c. 1, C. 22, q. 5,—p. 400; Huguccio ad c. 1, C. 22, q. 5, as quoted in Kuttner's *Schuldlehre*, p. 301, n. 4.

[8] Cf. *Glossa Ordinaria* ad c. 2, X, *De his quae vi*, I, 40. The exceptions were given in a verse:

Tutor, iudicium, dos, sacrum, copula, votum
Haec sex in vi facta, de iure scias fore nulla
cetera ius patitur, sed postea restituitur.

[9] Cf. Schmalzgrueber, lib. I, tit. XL, n. 2; Sporer, *Theologia Moralis Decalogalis et Sacramentalis* (3 vols., ed. Bierbaum, Paderbornae, 1897-1901), I, n. 156.

he be competent, if he threatens the evil in an illegitimate manner.[10] Fear is directly inflicted if it is intended to extort some particular action. It is inflicted indirectly when the one inflicting the fear does not intend a specific action to be performed by the one suffering the fear.[11]

According to its quantity fear is either grave or slight. Absolutely grave fear is such as would influence even a resolute man. Relatively grave fear is present when an evil is threatened which is light in itself but becomes grave due to the nature of the individual suffering the fear.

The only fear admitted in the Roman Law sources was absolutely grave fear, "qui cadere posset in virum constantem." This notion was prevalent also in canonical doctrine prior to the Council of Trent (1545-1563). Ioannes Andreae (1270-1348) took up the question of a lesser fear, but without acknowledging to it any power to render a contract voidable.[12] Later relatively grave fear came to be admitted as a cause rendering a contract rescissible.[13] Moreover, since this fear rendered the contract voidable because of the injury it entailed, the only fear ever admitted in this way was fear from without (*ab extrinseco*), i.e., such as was inflicted by a free human agent.[14]

This grave fear must be unjustly inflicted. It is disputed among the authors as to what type of unjust fear suffices to render the contract void or voidable. All admit that a fear which is substantially unjust (*quoad substantiam*) is sufficient. There are, however, some canonists who hold that fear which is unjust only because of the manner, i.e., in view of the concrete circumstances in which it is inflicted, is not sufficient to render the attempted contract either

[10] Beste, *Introductio in Codicem* (Collegeville, Minn.: St. John's Abbey Press, 1938), p. 159.

[11] Cf. Roberti, "De Metu Indirecto quoad Negotia Iuridica praesertim Matrimonium,"—*Apollinaris*, XI (1938), 559.

[12] Ioannes Andreae Bononiensis, *In Primum Decretalium Librum Commentaria* (Venetiis, 1581), Novella ad c. 5, X, *De his quae vi*, I, 40.

[13] Wernz, *Ius Decretalium*, VI, nn. 528-530.

[14] Cf. Laymann, *Theologia Moralis* (2 vols., Venetiis, 1719), lib. I, tract. II, cap. IV, nn. 5, 7, 8.

void or voidable.[15] However, the more common opinion holds that fear which is unjust, even though only *quoad modum,* is sufficient to render a contract rescissible. This opinion is certainly safe in practice.[16] The purpose of granting the rescissory action, or in the few exceptional cases the sanction of nullity, is to punish the evil action of the one threatening, or to protect the rights of the one suffering the fear. Surely then fear which is unjust because of circumstances (*quoad modum*), which implies an evil action on the part of the one threatening, and inflicts an injustice upon the one threatened, appears to be included among the causes granting a rescissory action or nullifying the binding force of the contract.[17]

A second difference of opinion on the question of the type of fear required concerns direct and indirect fear. Some of the authors maintain that the fear must be directly inflicted to extort this particular action before it gives grounds for a declaration of nullity or a rescissory action. The two basic arguments used by these authors are already given by Sanchez (1550-1610).[18] First, he argues, in such a case a man is not impelled to act by another, but rather by himself. This is so because no one demands a certain juridic action, but the contracting party voluntarily chooses it as a means of avoiding an evil to body or soul. His second argument maintains that the *involuntarium* found in this contractual act is not intended by the one inflicting the fear, but is only occasioned by his perversity.

There are many authors against this opinion.[19] These latter seem more logical in their analysis of the problem. In answer to the arguments of Sanchez as given above, it may be pointed out that in this instance of indirect fear there is really duress and there

[15] Cf. e.g., Noval, *De Processibus,* n. 430; Vermeersch-Creusen, *Epitome,* III, n. 111.

[16] Cf. Beste, *Introductio in Codicem,* p. 159; Sipos, *Enchiridion Iuris Canonici,* p. 94; Roberti, "De Metu Indirecto quoad Negotia Iuridica praesertim Matrimonium"—*Apollinaris,* XI (1938), 557-561.

[17] Roberti, *art. et loc. cit.*

[18] *De Sancto Matrimonii Sacramento Disputationum Libri Decem, in Tres Tomos Distributi* (Antverpiae, 1607), lib. IV, disp. XII, n. 3.

[19] Cf. among the pre-Code authors, Schmalzgrueber, lib. V, tit. XL, nn. 27 ss., and among post-Code authors, Beste, *Introductio in Codicem,* p. 159; Roberti, *art. cit.* in *Apollinaris,* XI (1938), 558.

is a true injury inflicted. For, as Savigny (1779-1861) points out, there is duress in such a case because of the very nature of such indirect fear.[20] Anyone suffering fear has actually a choice of only three courses of action, that is, either to place the act, or to resist the evil threatened, or to tolerate it. The difference between fear directly inflicted and that only indirectly inflicted consists in this that when it is directly inflicted there is only one act that can be placed, whereas in the case of indirect fear there is a choice of acts that can be placed to escape the evil. Evidently if one of these acts would not entail a grave evil, the fear is not grave. However, if all the acts constitute grave evils, and the one suffering the fear chooses the lesser evil, then there is certainly a case of duress in regard to this act. For the will is thus conditionally forced to this action.

It must also be stressed that there is actual injury in case of such indirect fear. For even though the act placed is chosen as the lesser evil, there is a true causal relation between the fear and the act. Such fear must be said to be virtually the cause of all the acts which can be done to escape the evil. If the one suffering the fear selects a lesser evil, no one can affirm that the injury ceases in repect to this act.[21] The Code itself seems to indicate that indirect fear offers sufficlent grounds for the rescinding of a contract. In enumerating the conditions necessary for a rescinding of contracts, etc., canon 103, § 2, speaks simply of "grave fear, unjustly inflicted." [22] The Code does not require any other condition in the particular canons dealing with the individual contracts.[23]

The fear, then, which gives the right to propose the exception of fear must be grave, either absolutely or relatively. It must be fear

[20] *Sistema del Diritto Romano Attuale* (versio V. Torino, Scialoia, 1892), III, § 114, pp. 126-127.

[21] Cf. Roberti, *art. cit.* in *Apollinaris,* XI (1938), 558.

[22] "Actus positi ex metu gravi et iniuste incusso . . . valent, . . . sed possunt . . . rescindi . . . "—canon 103, § 2; cf. also canon 1684, § 1.

[23] Cf. canons 1851; 214, § 1; 542, § 1; 572, § 1, n. 4; 1807, § 1 (this last canon may seem to demand more to invalidate a marriage, but the Code is here considering the end of the one suffering the fear, not the one inflicting it, when it adds "a quo ut quis se liberet eligere cogatur matrimonium"); 1307, § 3. Cf. also Roberti, *De Processibus,* n. 247.

from without, *inflicted* by a free human agent, and must be unjust at least *quoad modum*. And, finally, it suffices that it be indirectly inflicted.

The Code speaks of the possibility of the exception if the plaintiff is the one who caused the fear.[24] Some authors hold that the exception can therefore be raised only against the one responsible for the fear.[25] Although this may seem to be indicated in the wording of the canon, it seems more logical that an exception could be raised against any plaintiff who sues for the execution of an act or contract entered through grave fear. For there is a real injury involved in such a case and there is duress. Moreover, since the contract is rescissible in such a case, there must be an exception possible in order to allow the defendant to protect his right of asking for a rescissory action.[26]

Ordinarily in contentious cases such an exception of fear would have to be placed by the parties themselves. However, if the issue concerns a question involving the common good, the judge may advert to this exception of fear *ex officio*.[27]

The purpose of a peremptory exception such as that of fear is to elide the juridical action brought against the one claiming the exception. In the instance of a suit brought by a plaintiff who inflicted unjust fear upon the other party, the exception of fear serves to prevent the execution of the act demanded by the plaintiff. However, it must be stressed that the proving of such an exception does not secure the condemnation of the plaintiff in favor of the defendant. In other words, the rescissible contract is not thereby rescinded, since the defendant has not actually asked for this. The only way he can petition this is by means of an action if the time for such has not elapsed. This serves to illustrate clearly an important difference between a court action and a judicial exception.[28]

[24] "Si is qui metum intulit . . . urgeat actus vel contractus executionem. . . ." Canon 1686.

[25] Cf., e. g., Coronata, *Institutiones*, n. 1214.

[26] Cf. Roberti, *art. cit.* in *Apollinaris*, XI (1938), 559. Vermeersch-Creusen (*Epitome*, III, n. 115) maintain that in such a case there is an opportunity of sequestration of goods or injunction of the exercise of rights.

[27] Canon 1618.

[28] Cf. Noval, *De Processibus*, n. 342.

This exception of fear is termed a simple peremptory exception, in counter-distinction to the other peremptory exceptions termed *litis finitae*. The law requires that such simple peremptory exceptions be settled along with the principal cause as an incidental question. Consequently it must be placed after the joinder of issue.[29] And correspondingly it must be placed before the definitive sentence.[30] Since such an exception pertains to the merits of the cause it may not be placed after the definitive sentence. However, even after such a sentence, grave fear can constitute grounds for employing the remedy of appeal or for invoking a *restitutio in integrum*.[31]

It seems that an interlocutory sentence should be required to settle this exception, since an extensive investigation may be required to establish the facts. However, if the matter is of little importance, or if the parties so agree, a mere decree will suffice.[32]

Article 2. Fraud

Canon 1686 mentions the right to cite the exception of fraud (deceit) when the deceived party is sued for the execution of the act or contract by a plaintiff who practiced the deceit.[33] The term *dolus* used in the canon is taken from Roman Law sources. Here the term was used in two different meanings. In criminal law *dolus* meant the deliberate violation of the law.[34] In civil matters the term *dolus* came to include every kind of malicious act perpetrated to the disadvantage of another person, although the original meaning included only fraudulent misrepresentation.[35] Although the term

[29] Canon 1629, § 2.

[30] Cf. Roberti, *De Processibus*, n. 158.

[31] Canon 1687.

[32] Wernz-Vidal, *Ius Canonicum*, VI, n. 548; Coronata, *Institutiones*, n. 1372.

[33] "Si is qui . . . dolum patravit, urgeat actus vel contractus executionem, parti . . . deceptae competit exceptio . . . doli."

[34] E. g., D. (48.12) (2. 1) (*Lex Iulia de Annona*); D. (48.10) (9. 2) (*Lex Cornelia de Falsis*).

[35] Cf. Schulz, *Principles of Roman Law* (Oxford: Clarendon Press, 1936), pp. 45-46; Swoboda, *Ignorance in Relation to the Imputability of Delicts*, The Catholic University of America Canon Law Studies, n. 143 (Washington D. C.: The Catholic University of America Press, 1941), p. 30.

could be understood in a good sense to indicate cleverness, etc.,[36] it has come to be used only in a pejorative sense in law. This latter concept is described in Roman Law as a cunning, an intrigue, or trickery to circumvent, dupe or deceive the other person.[37] The expression *dolus* is translated into English as fraud or deceit. It is in this sense that *dolus* is understood in those canons of the Code which employ it in regard to civil matters.[38]

This fraud or deceit is either substantial or accidental. Substantial fraud is such as concerns the essential elements of an act or object, or which regards a condition placed as *sine qua non*. Accidental fraud is that which concerns the incidental qualities of an act or an object. This latter fraud may be either antecedent (*dans causam*) or concomitant and co-incidental. Antecedent fraud is had whenever the agent would not have made the contract, etc., if he knew of the fraud. If he would be ready to go through with the act or contract even though he knew of the fraud the accidental fraud is then co-incidental.[39]

Any fraud by which one of the contracting parties falls into a substantial error regarding the object of the contract renders the business pact or contract null and void by reason of the natural law. The reason for this lies in the fact that a substantial error in either of the contracting parties absolutely excludes mutual consent in the same object, which consent is essential to every contract. In other business pacts it excludes the consent of the one upon whose will the pact depends.

As a general rule fraud which produces only an accidental error does not void a contract or other pact either from the natural law, canon law or civil enactment. Such is the case even if the error is antecedent and gives rise to the contract. In such instances the fraud does not take away the consent to the substance of the act or contract.[40] However, the Church can by positive enactment render

[36] Cf. D. (4.3) (1. 3).

[37] D. (4.3) (1. 2).

[38] Canons 103; 185; 542; 572; 1684; 1685; 1686. Cf. Roberti, *De Processibus*, I, n. 246; Noval, *De Iudiciis*, n. 340.

[39] Cf. Beste, *Introductio in Codicem*, p. 157.

[40] Cf. Wernz-Vidal, *Ius Canonicum*, VI, p. 267.

even such acts null. For it is the duty of the law to protect the liberty of the individual, and the principles of equity and justice demand that the one who suffers an injury be indemnified. Thus the Church generally grants a rescissory action to anyone injured by fraud which produces accidental error; but in some exceptional instances, expressly stated in law, it renders the act void from the beginning.[41] These exceptional cases contained in the law are the following: the vote of an elector who is thus deceived; [42] the renouncing of an ecclesiastical office;[43] entrance into the novitiate;[44] religious profession.[45]

In other cases a rescissory action is granted to those who are deceived by such fraud as produces an accidental error. All authors admit this is the case of the contract or pact actually arising from the error thus produced. The reason for this is clear. As indicated above, the one deceiving, who thus induces the other party to enter a contract, injures his liberty and unjustly inflicts an injury upon him. This cannot be remedied unless full liberty and compensation for damages are restored to the one deceived. This can be done only by a declaration of nullity in those cases where the act or contract is null before the law, or by a rescissory action without prejudice to the action for damages provided for in canon 2210, § 1, 2°. This of course does not apply to those acts which by divine, positive, or natural law cannot be voided, as for example, validity of orders.

There is a dispute among canonists as to whether this nullity or rescissory action would obtain also in the case of fraud which produces only incidental (concomitant) error. Some deny this because they do not see a sufficient reason for it in a mere incidental fraud. They argue that the party would have performed the act or made the contract anyway, even though under different conditions, and hence it is sufficient if they are indemnified for any loss they have sus-

[41] Cf. Beste, *Introductio in Codicem,* p. 158.

[42] Canon 169, § 1.

[43] Canon 185.

[44] Canon 542, 1°.

[45] Canon 572, § 1, 4°.

tained.[46] Many post-code authors, however, hold that this rescissory action or declaration of nullity, as the case may be, is available also to the one deceived, even when the error is only concomitant or incidental.[47]

The Code itself does not distinguish between antecedent and incidental or concomitant error, nor does it state that the rights of the one deceived are satisfied as long as he is compensated for the damage done. The argument from pre-Code authorities is not at all conclusive because precisely in this section the Code does not admit many distinctions of the previous law.[48] Consequently the latter opinion seems altogether safe in practice.

In all cases wherein the act is rescissible because of deceit, the defendant can raise the *exceptio doli* when the plaintiff demands the execution of this act or contract. The effect of this exception, as in the case of the exception of fear, is to remove the juridical action brought against the one who was deceived. In this way it prevents the execution of the act demanded by the plaintiff. The contract or pact, however, is not actually rescinded by a favorable judgment on this exception. The contract or pact is judged rescissible, not rescinded.

The authors usually stress rescissible contracts when treating the exception of *dolus*. But when the contract is not merely rescissible but actually null from the beginning, a defendant can evidently make use of such an exception. For since every right can be enforced not only by action in court, unless the contrary is explicitly stated, but also by exception, which is always available and of its very nature perpetual, an exception would evidently be allowed here.[49] In such a case, however, the effect of the exception would

[46] Cf. Roberti, *De Processibus,* I, n. 246; Beste, *Introductio in Codicem,* p. 159; Bieter, "The Canon Law on Deceit"—*ER,* LVI (1922), 42-51. This opinion seems to have been held quite generally by pre-Code authors. Cf., e. g., Pirhing, lib. II, tit. XIV, n. 3; Schmalzgrueber, lib. II, tit. XIV, n. 19; Wernz, *Ius Decretalium,* V, 407.

[47] Cf. Wernz-Vidal, *Ius Decretalium,* VI, p. 268; Noval, *De Processibus,* n. 340; Vermeersch-Creusen, *Epitome,* III, n. 112.

[48] Cf. Wernz-Vidal, *Ius Canonicum,* VI, p. 268.

[49] Canon 1667.

evidently differ from that of the usual ***exceptio doli accidentalis.*** Although primarily intended to remove the juridical action, a favorable judgment on such an exception would serve as a declarative sentence of the nullity of the contract or pact. Here it is not a question of declaring this act rescissible, but of declaring it actually null from the beginning.[50]

As in the case of the exception of fear, this exception of fraud can be raised against any plaintiff who sues for the execution of an act or contract entered because of fraud.[51] And such an exception, though ordinarily to be placed by the parties themselves, must be adverted to by the judge *ex officio* if the issue concerns a question involving the common good.[52] This exception may also be placed by the heirs of the parties.[53]

The exception of *dolus* is another simple peremptory exception to be settled along with the principal cause as an incidental question. Thus, as in the case of the exception of fear,[54] it should be placed after the joinder of issue,[55] and may not be placed after the definitive sentence. However, fraud that renders a contract rescissible or null from the beginning is sufficient ground for employing the remedy of appeal or for invoking ***restitutio in integrum,*** even after a definitive sentence.[56]

It seems that an interlocutory sentence should be required to settle this exception, because an extensive investigation may be required to settle it. However, if the matter is of little importance, or if the parties so agree, a mere decree would suffice.[57]

[50] Cf. canon 1552, § 2, 1°: "Obiectum iudicii sunt: 1° Personarum physicarum vel moralium . . . facta iuridica declaranda. . . ."

[51] Cf. *supra,* p. 129.

[52] Canon 1618.

[53] Cf. De Angelis, *Praelectiones,* lib. II, tit. XIV, 299; Reiffenstuel, lib. II, tit. XIV, nn. 30-31.

[54] Cf. *supra,* p. 139.

[55] Canon 1629, § 2.

[56] Canon 1687. Cf. *supra,* p. 140; Król, *The Defendant in Contentious Trials,* p. 114; Roberti, *De Processibus,* n. 158.

[57] Cf. Wernz-Vidal, *Ius Canonicum,* VI, n. 548; Coronata, *Institutiones,* n. 1372.

Article 3. Error

The Code itself does not speak of an exception of error. From the general principle of canon 1667, however, it must be concluded that when there is a right involved there is also an exception to protect it.[58] Blat, while admitting that such is the case in theory, maintains that in practice there is no opportunity for an exception of error. His argument is that since the rescissory action is granted only when the person has suffered damages amounting to over one-half the amount involved in the contract,[59] it is presupposed that the contract has been executed and thus there is no chance for an exception such as is granted in the case of fear or fraud.[60] However, there is surely an exception when the error renders the act or contract null, and the effect of this exception will be the same as that of the exception of fraud in those cases wherein fraud invalidates the act or contract. In the case of accidental error, it seems that a defendant can always propose the exception of error when the plaintiff sues for the execution of an act or contract entered through accidental error and whose execution would entail losing over one-half the amount of the contract on the part of the defendant. If a favorable judgment is received on this exception it would stop the action of the plaintiff and the contract would seemingly be judged rescissible.[61]

The manner of proving and settling this exception, and also the type of decree or sentence required, will follow the manner of the exceptions of fear and fraud.[62]

Article 4. Prescription

Prescription as an exception may be defined as a peremptory exception taking its substance from a time set by law, in consequence

[58] "Quodlibet ius . . . munitur . . . exceptione, quae semper competit et est suapte natura perpetua."

[59] Canon 1684, § 2.

[60] *Commentarium Textus Codicis Iuris Canonici, Liber IV, De Processibus,* n. 173, p. 204.

[61] Roberti (*De Processibus,* n. 383) indicates the above in stating that there is an exception of error corresponding to the rescissory action for error.

[62] Cf. *supra,* pp. 140, 148.

of which a possessor in good faith can repel in court the owner of the thing possessed when the latter attempts to establish his right.[63] The principle of prescription is based on the fact that it is expedient for the common good that ownership of all things be definitely determined.[64]

Prescription may be *acquisitive (usucapio)*, namely, when a right is acquired positively. It is *liberative* or *extinctive* when a person is freed from some duty or obligation.[65] The Code of Canon Law deals with *acquisitive* prescription in canons 1508-1512, with *liberative* prescription in canons 1701-1705.

A. *Acquisitive Prescription*

The general norms for prescription are determined by the civil statutes with particular limitations imposed by the Church law.[66]

The following conditions are required for valid prescription: (1) matter or right capable of being obtained by means of legal prescription; (2) good faith on the part of the one who employs the agency of prescription; (3) a just title; (4) possession; (5) the lapse of the required time.[67]

Anything in itself is capable of being obtained through the agency of prescription provided that the natural or positive law does not indicate otherwise.[68] The following are stated in the Code as being excluded: (1) provisions of the divine law, both natural and positive; (2) things which may be obtained only by apostolic privilege; (3) spiritual rights which lay persons are not qualified to possess when the prescriptive matter concerns a layman; (4) the certain and

[63] De Angelis, *Praelectiones*, lib. II, tit. XXVI, 180; Roberti, *De Processibus*, I, n. 299; Noval, *De Iudiciis*, n. 372; Schmalzgrueber, lib. II, tit. XXVI, nn. 1-10.

[64] Noval, *De Iudiciis*, n. 372.

[65] Coronata, *Compendium Iuris Canonici* (2 vols., Taurini: 1938), n. 1681 (hereafter cited *Compendium*).

[66] Canon 1508.

[67] Canons 1508-1512; De Angelis, *Praelectiones*, lib. II, tit. XXVI, p. 185; Coronata, *Compendium*, nn. 1681-1688; De Meester, *Compendium*, nn. 1461-1463.

[68] De Meester, *Compendium*, n. 1461.

unquestioned boundaries of ecclesiastical provinces, dioceses, parishes, viçariates apostolic and prefectures apostolic, abbacies and prelacies *nullius*; (5) alms or Mass stipends and obligations; (6) ecclesiastical benefices obtained without title; (7) the right of canonical visitation and obedience; (8) the payment of the cathedraticum.[69]

Sacred things owned by private persons may be objects which can fall within the potential orbit of legal prescription, but they may not be used for profane purposes; if they have lost their consecration or blessing they may be obtained through the agency of legal prescription for profane but not for sordid use.[70] Sacred things which do not belong to private persons cannot be acquired through the agency of legal prescription by a private person; in these, however, moral persons may prescribe against other moral persons.[71]

Good faith is required for every kind and for every moment of the prescription.[72] A buyer in good faith is described as one who does not know that a thing belongs to another, or who thinks that the one who sold the property had the right to do so.[73]

A just title is required [74] because it is the source of good faith, the foundation of a just possession, and also is described as the cause or reason which is sufficient in itself to transfer ownership or to provide a condition for the realization of an operative legal prescription.[75] Among the titles are sale, inheritance, gift and legacy.[76]

[69] Canon 1509. Cf. Benedictus XIV, ep. *"Declarasti,"* 16 mart. 1746—*Fontes*, n. 365; S.C.C., *Lucana.*, 9 ian. 1825—*Fontes*, n. 3991; Pirhing, lib. II, tit. XXVI, n. 12; Schmalzgrueber, lib. II, tit. XXVI, n. 33.

[70] Canon 1510, § 1.

[71] Canon 1510, § 2.

[72] Canon 1512. Cf. c. 20, X, *de prescriptionibus*, II, 26.

[73] C. 17, X, *de prescriptionibus*, II, 26; Schmalzgrueber, lib. II, tit. XXVI, n. 55; Roberti, *De Processibus*, n. 227; Coronata, *Compendium*, n. 1685.

[74] C. 17, X, *de prescriptionibus*, II, 26; Schmalzgrueber, lib. II, tit. XXVI, n. 55; Coronata, *Compendium*, n. 1684. A just title, which the Romans called the *iusta causa usucapionis*, is the fact or series of facts by which it may be demonstrated that the actual possessor entered into possession without injury to the former possessor. Cf. Coronata, *loc. cit.*

[75] Schmalzgrueber, lib. II, tit. XXVI, nn. 84, 85; Coronata, *loc. cit.*

[76] De Angelis, *Praelectiones*, lib. II, tit. XXVI, 208.

A title may be true, colored, putative, or presumed. A true title is had when all things necessary for transferring ownership are present in fact. A colored title is had when the transferring of the ownership really takes place but remains without operative effect on account of some hidden defect. Putative and presumed titles do not accomplish a transfer of ownership on account of some hidden defect. In the cases of putative and presumed titles no title is present and therefore also no transfer of ownership is effected. In the one case the title is erroneously thought to be present, in the other case the title is unjustifiably anticipated to exist.[77]

Possession is described as the holding of a thing as one's own with the aid of the law. It is required to be continuous and uninterrupted. It must also be peaceful, manifest, unequivocal and exercised in one's own name or in the name of another.[78]

Real and valuable movable property, rights and personal or real actions which pertain to the Holy See may be effectively touched by means of the legal agency of prescription only after 100 years of adverse possession.[79] Thirty years' possession is necessary for the effective operation of legal prescription against other ecclesiastical moral persons.[80] These are the only specifications with regard to time that are enacted in the Code. The civil statutes are to be followed in other cases.[81]

The general statutory provisions for the acquiring of real property by means of the title of adverse possession have varied time specifications in the various States of the United States: Alabama, ten years; Arizona, two years; Arkansas, seven years; California, five years; Colorado, eighteen years; Connecticut, fifteen years; Delaware, twenty years; District of Columbia, fifteen years; Florida, seven years; Georgia, twenty years; Idaho, five years; Illinois, twenty years; Indiana, twenty years; Iowa, ten years; Kansas, fif-

[77] Schmalzgrueber, lib. II, tit. XXVI, nn. 86, 87; De Angelis, *Praelectiones*, lib. II, tit. XXVI, 208, 209; Coronata, *Compendium*, n. 1684.

[78] Coronata, *Compendium*, n. 1687.

[79] Canon 1511, § 1. Cf. Benedictus XIV, *const.* "*Ad honorandam,*" 27 mart. 1752—*Fontes*, n. 420.

[80] Canon 1511, § 2.

[81] Canon 1508.

teen years; Kentucky, fifteen years; Louisiana, two years with all conditions present, thirty years, without need of title and regardless of good faith; Maine, twenty years; Maryland, twenty years; Massachusetts, twenty years; Michigan, fifteen years; Minnesota, fifteen years; Mississippi, ten years; Missouri, ten years; Montana, ten years; Nebraska, ten years; Nevada, five years; New Hampshire, twenty years; New Jersey, thirty years; New Mexico, ten years; New York, fifteen years; North Carolina, twenty years; North Dakota, twenty years; Ohio, twenty-one years; Oklahoma, fifteen years; Oregon, ten years; Pennsylvania, twenty-one years; Rhode Island, ten years; South Carolina, ten years; South Dakota, twenty years; Tennessee, seven years; Texas, five years; Utah, seven years; Vermont, fifteen years; Virginia, fifteen years for land east of the Allegheny Mountains, ten years for land west of the Alleghany Mountains; Washington, ten years; West Virginia, ten years; Wisconsin, twenty years; Wyoming, ten years.[82]

B. *Liberative Prescription*

Actions are said to be extinguished when the right to prosecute a cause in court has been completely lost.[83]

In contentious causes, real and personal actions may be extinguished by legal prescription according to the civil statues; actions, however, which concern the state of persons are never extinguished.[84] The state of persons here considered involves an individual's status as a citizen or as a member of the Church,[85] or it refers to the less

[82] These are merely the general references with regard to the time element in the various States. For additional variations of the law the reader may consult the various State statutes or the *Martindale-Hubbell Law Directory* (Summit, N. J.: Martindale-Hubbell, Inc., 1943), II. There is no pagination indicated in this work, but the facts may be found under the title of "Adverse Possession" in connection with the list under the headings of the various States.

[83] Coronata, *Institutiones*, n. 1230; Wernz-Vidal, *Ius Canonicum*, VI, n. 358.

[84] Canon 1701.

[85] Canons 87, 682.

general canonical states of Christians as married, clerical or religious.[86]

All the limitations imposed by canons 1508-1512 as indicated above apply to liberative as well as acquisitive prescription.[87] However, in liberative prescription a title is not required and positive possession is not necessary; the possession of liberty is sufficient.[88]

Besides those periods of time already indicated as being required for acquisitive prescription specific time limitations with regard to certain actions are stated as follows: (1) actions concerning the nullity of a sentence can be proposed within thirty years; [89] (2) certain actions which are rescissory as a result of error are outlawed within two years; [90] (3) the action of *restitutio in integrum* must be employed within four years; [91] (4) the action of retaining possession [92] and the action of regaining possession [93] are not admitted after a year has elapsed.

Criminal suits may not be proposed after the lapse of a three-year period; actions based on injuries lapse after one year; five years is the time limit for actions introduced as the result of qualified delicts against the sixth and seventh commandments; actions based on simony and homicide lapse only after a ten-year period.[94]

Prescription in contentious causes starts at the moment when an

[86] Lega, *De Iudiciis Ecclesiasticis,* I, n. 306; Vermeersch-Creusen, *Epitome,* III, n. 135; Noval, *De Iudiciis,* n. 375; Wernz-Vidal, *Ius Canonicum,* VI, n. 361; Augustine, *Commentary,* VII, 149.

[87] Canon 1701. Cf. Noval, *De Iudiciis,* n. 374; Roberti, *De Processibus,* n. 227.

[88] Coronata, *Institutiones,* n. 1231.

[89] Canon 1893, § 2.

[90] "Si quis motus metu gravi iniuste incusso, vel dolo circumventus actum posuerit vel contractum inierit qui ipso iure non sit nullus, poterit, metu vel dolo probato, obtinere actus vel contractus rescissionem actione quae vocatur rescissoria."—Canon 1684, § 1. "Eadem actione intra biennium uti potest, qui gravem ex contractu laesionem ultra dimidium ex errore passus est."—Canon 1684, § 2.

[91] Canon 1688.

[92] Canon 1695, § 2.

[93] Canon 1698, § 2.

[94] Canon 1703.

action could have been proposed, in criminal causes from the day the delict was perpetrated.[95]

The Code of Canon Law provides that the civil law of the place is to be followed as a norm also in the matter of liberative prescription.[96]

The various states have various statutory provisions regarding the time required for the extinction of actions: [97]

Alabama: ten years: actions on sealed instruments; six years: actions for trespass to persons on or to personal or real property; five years: actions founded on equities or redemption; three years: actions to recover money due an open or unliquidated account.

Arizona: ten years: actions to recover real estate as against person having peaceable and adverse possession thereof and cultivating or using the same; six years: actions on any written instrument, sealed or unsealed, executed within the state; five years: actions to recover real estate as against person in peaceable possession thereof, cultivating or using and paying taxes on the same; four years: on written instrument, sealed or unsealed, executed without the state; three years: to recover real estate as against a person in peaceable and adverse possession under title or color of title, for debt not evidenced by writing; two years: to recover possession of real estate as against person who claims right of possession only; for injury to real or personal property; for wrongful taking or detention of personal property; for trespass or conversion; for forcible entry and detainer; for personal injury; one year: for libel, slander.

Arkansas: ten years: actions on judgments; eight years: on bonds of executors or administrators; seven years: on recovery of real property; five years: on promissory notes and other instruments in writing, sealed or unsealed; all actions not otherwise provided for;

[95] Canon 1705, § 1.

[96] Canons 1701; 1508.

[97] *The Martindale-Hubbell Law Directory* is the source for the information which follows. There is no pagination indicated in this work, but one may find the facts by consulting the title "Limitation of Actions" under the general headings of the various States. Only the principal items are cited here. The time specified represents the limit for placing an action; by the lapse of a longer time the action will be extinguished by prescription.

three years: on open accounts; express or implied contracts not in writing; for trespass on lands; one year: for assault and battery, slander.

California: ten years: real property actions by the state; bonds and coupons issued by the state; five years: real property actions by others than the state; four years: any contract, obligation or liability founded upon an instrument in writing; any action not otherwise provided for; three years: on any liability created by statute; two years: any contract, obligation or liability not founded upon an instrument in writing; one year: to most injuries to person or character.

Colorado: eighteen years: to recover real property where there is no other statutory limitation; fifteen years: to foreclose a mortgage; six years: actions on a debt on any contract or liability in writing; three years: action on a contract not otherwise covered; one year: assault and battery, libel or slander.

Connecticut: seventeen years: on note or other written contract under seal; fifteen years: to recover real property; six years: on unsealed negotiable promissory note or other written contract; three years: on express oral contract; for torts except those otherwise specified; one year: for death, for negligent injury to person or property.

Delaware: six years: actions on bills or notes, or an acknowledgment under the hand of the party of a subsisting demand; three years: actions on trespass, replevin, detinue, debt not founded upon a record or specialty; one year: actions for personal injuries.

District of Columbia: fifteen years: actions on real property; twelve years: on any bond or single bill other than executors' and administrators' bonds; five years: on executors' and administrators' bonds; three years: on any simple contract, express or implied, for recovery of damages, for injury to real or personal property, or damages for its unlawful detention; one year: for any statutory penalty.

Florida: twenty years: on judgment or decree of court record; on note or other contract under seal; five years: on note or other contract in writing not under seal; four years: for relief not specifically provided for; three years: on liability created by statute, other than penalty or forfeiture; for trespass on real property; for taking, detaining or injuring any goods or chattels, including actions for the recovery of any specific personal property; two years: for libel, slander, assault and battery.

Georgia: twenty years: on bond, note or other instrument under seal; ten years: on domestic judgment; six years: on promissory note, bill of exchange or other simple contract in writing; four years: on open account or for breach of contract not in writing; for trespass on or damage to realty or injury to personalty; for action *ex contractu* for which no other period is prescribed; two years: for injury to person; one year: for injury to reputation.

Idaho: five years: to recover real estate; on written obligations, sealed or unsealed; four years: for obligations not in writing; on an open account; on mutual accounts; on actions for which no other limitation is prescribed; three years: on statutory liability; for injury to personal or real property; to recover possession of personal property; two years: for personal injuries, for death, libel, slander, assault and battery.

Illinois: ten years: actions on bonds, notes, written contracts and other evidences in writing, sealed or unsealed; five years: for oral contracts, implied promises, awards of arbitration; for actions to recover possession of, for injuries to and for detention or conversion of personal property; for actions not otherwise provided for.

Indiana: thirty-five years: to rectify certain defects in record title; twenty years: on judgment of courts of record; for recovery of real property; on contracts in writing, sealed or unsealed; on real estate mortgages or vendors' liens on real estate; fifteen years: on judgment of courts not of record; ten years: on promissory notes, bills of exchange and other written contracts, sealed or unsealed, for payment of money; six years: on accounts not in writing; for use, rent or profits of real property; for recovery of personal property and damages for detention thereof; two years: for injuries to person or character.

Iowa: ten years: to recover real property; on written contract, sealed or unsealed; five years: on unwritten contract; for injury to real or personal property; to recover possession of personal property; two years: to enforce mechanic's lien; for injuries to person or reputation.

Kansas: fifteen years: to recover real property except where there are specific limitations; five years: on agreement, contract or promise in writing, sealed or unsealed; on judgment; on any action for which there is no other specification; three years: on a contract not in writing; on a liability created by statute, other than penalty or forfeiture; two years: for trespass on real property; for taking, detaining or injuring personal property; for injury of rights of another not arising from contract; one year: for libel, slander, assault and battery.

Kentucky: fifteen years: to recover real estate; on judgment or decree; on written contract or bond, sealed or unsealed; ten years: action for which no other limitation is prescribed; five years: action on contract not in writing, express or implied; for injury to real or personal property or to recover possession of personal property or damages for its detention; one year: for action for personal injury or death, libel and slander.

Louisiana: ten years: on all personal actions, except those otherwise indicated; five years: actions on bills of exchange, notes payable to order of bearer, except bank notes; those on all effects negotiable or transferable by endorsement or delivery; one year: on all tort actions.

Maine: twenty years: on witnessed promissory notes; on all contracts not otherwise limited; six years: on contract or liability not under seal; for rent; for waste; for trespass; for injury to chattels; two years: for assault and battery, libel, slander or death.

Maryland: twenty years: to recover real property; twelve years: on note, bond or other written contract not under seal; on oral contract; on account; for injury to real or personal property; to recover possession of personal property; for negligent personal injury; for tort not otherwise limited; one year: for libel, slander, assault and battery.

Massachusetts: twenty years: on real actions; six years: actions on contracts under seal, on bills, and notes; actions of replevin; actions of tort, except those mentioned otherwise; two years: assault, battery, slander; one year: libel.

Michigan: fifteen years: on mortgages; six years: for personal actions unless specified otherwise; two years: assault and battery; one year: libel and slander.

Minnesota: fifteen years: for recovery of real estate or foreclosure of mortgage; six years: contract or other obligation, express or implied; liability created by statute except penalty or forfeiture; trespass on or injury to real property; taking, detaining or injuring personal property and actions for the specific recovery thereof; two years: for libel, slander, assault, battery or other tort resulting in personal injury.

Mississippi: ten years: to recover real property; six years: on note or other written contract, sealed or unsealed; for injury to real or personal property; for personal injury; for death; for action for which no other period is prescribed; three years: to recover possession of personal property; on unwritten contract or open account or account stated but not acknowledged in writing; one year: for libel, slander, assault and battery.

Missouri: ten years: on any instrument in writing, sealed or unsealed for the payment of money or property except as herein stated; five years: on contracts, obligations or liabilities, express or implied; for trespass or injury to real estate; for taking, detaining or injuring any goods or chattels and actions for the recovery of specific personal property, or for any other injury to the person or rights of another, not arising from contract and not otherwise enumerated; two years: for libel, slander, assault and battery.

Montana: ten years: for the recovery of real property; eight years: on contract, obligation or liability founded upon an instrument in writing, sealed or unsealed; five years: on an account or promise not founded upon an instrument in writing; two years: libel, slander assault and battery; action for trespass on real or personal property; taking, detaining or injuring any goods or chattel including actions for the specific recovery of personal property.

Nebraska: ten years: to recover real estate; five years: on specialty or any agreement, contract or promise in writing, express or implied; four years: on contract not in writing, express or implied; for taking, detaining or injuring personal property; one year: for libel, slander, assault and battery.

Nevada: five years: to recover real property; four years: on accounts; on contracts, obligations or liabilities not founded upon instruments in writing; for any action not otherwise specified; three years: for waste or trespass upon real property; for taking, detaining or injuring goods or chattel; two years: for libel, slander, assault and battery.

New Hampshire: twenty years: to recover real property; actions of debt upon judgments, recognizances and contracts under seal; six years: for all personal actions, except those otherwise specified; two years: libel, slander and actions of trespass to the person.

New Jersey: twenty years: for recovery of realty; six years: actions of trespass on land, actions regarding personal property; on contract without specialty; for rent on parol demise; two years: actions for injuries to persons; one year: libel or slander.

New Mexico: ten years: to recover real estate; six years: actions upon bonds, promissory notes or other contracts in writing; four years: on accounts, unwritten contracts, injuries to real or personal property; one year: for personal injury or death.

New York: forty years: for real property; ten years: action for which no other time is specified; six years: on contract, express or implied, other than judgment; on sealed instrument; to recover chattel; for injury to person except as otherwise provided; three years: for assault and battery; one year: for libel, slander.

North Carolina: twenty years: to recover real property; ten years: action upon sealed instrument against the principal thereto; for foreclosure or mortgage; three years: action on a contract or an obligation or liability arising out of a contract, express or implied; action upon a liability created by statute; action for trespass upon real property; one year: libel, assault and battery.

North Dakota: twenty years: to recover real property; ten years: on contract contained in conveyance or instrument affecting title to realty; for mortgage foreclosure; for an action not otherwise provided for; six years: on a contract (oral or written, sealed or unsealed), obligation or liability not otherwise provided for; for trespass or injury to real property; for taking, detaining or injuring chattels or for recovery of possession thereof; for injury to person or persons not based on contract; two years: for slander, libel, assault and battery.

Ohio: twenty-one years: to recover real property; fifteen years: on written contract, sealed or unsealed; ten years: on any action not otherwise provided for; six years: on a contract not in writing, express or implied; on liability created by statute other than penalty or forfeiture; four years: for trespass on real property; for taking or detaining personal property or for recovery thereof; for injury to rights of plaintiff not arising from contract; two years: for bodily injury or injury to personal property; one year: for libel, slander, assault and battery.

Oklahoma: fifteen years: for recovery of real property not otherwise provided for; five years: for recovery of real property sold under process or order of the court; three years: on contracts not in writing; on accounts stated or open accounts; two years: for trespass on real property; for taking, detaining or injuring personal property; one year: for libel, slander, assault and battery

Oregon: ten years: to recover real property; on sealed instruments; on any action not otherwise provided for; six years: on express or implied contracts not under seal, whether written or oral; for injury to real or personal property; five years: on contract for sale of real property; two years: for personal injury or other personal tort except libel or slander; one year: for libel or slander.

Pennsylvania: twenty-one years: to recover real property; twenty years: actions on judgment, mortgages and other instruments under seal; six years: actions on contracts, notes and instruments not under seal, whether written or oral; for trespass on real or personal property or to recover possession of personal property; for actions for which no other time is specified; two years: for trespass to person where injury does not result in death; one year: for libel and slander.

Rhode Island: twenty years: actions of covenant; on debt, unless otherwise provided for; on note or other written contract under seal; six years: on unsealed note or other written contract; on oral contract; four years: for trespass, except for injuries to person; two years: for personal injury or death; one year: for slander.

South Carolina: forty years: to recover real property; twenty years: on bond or other contract in writing secured by mortgage or real property; on sealed instrument other than sealed note or personal bond for payment of money only; ten years: actions for relief not otherwise provided for; for trespass upon or damage to personal property; two years: for libel, slander, assault and battery.

South Dakota: twenty years: to recover real property, except in cases otherwise indicated; on sealed instruments; fifteen years: to foreclose any real estate mortgage by action or advertisement; six years: on contract, express or implied, not otherwise provided for: for trespass on real property; three years: for personal injury; two years: for libel, slander, assault and battery.

Tennessee: ten years: to enforce mortgage or deed of trust; any action not otherwise provided for; seven years: to recover real property; six years: on bond, note, bill of exchange or other written contract, sealed or unsealed; on oral or implied contract; on account; three years: for injury to real or personal property; for detention or conversion of personal property; one year: for injury to person, death or libel.

Texas: five years: to recover real property; four years: on contracts in writing; two years: for injuries to person or property; on contracts not in writing; for death; for detaining personal property; one year: injuries to character or reputation.

Utah: seven years: to recover real property; six years: on contract, obligation or liability founded on an instrument in writing (no distinction between sealed and unsealed instruments); on account stated in writing; four years on contract, obligation or liability not founded upon an instrument in writing; for personal injury; for actions for which no other period is provided; three years: for waste or trespass on real property; for taking, detaining or injuring personal property; two years: for death; one year: for libel, slander, assault and battery.

Vermont: fifteen years: for recovery of real estate; fourteen years: on promissory note signed in the presence of an attesting witness; eight years: on judgment or covenant of warranty on note or other written contract under seal; six years: on note or other written contract not under seal; on oral or implied contract obligation or liability; for trespass or injury to personal property; for recovery of personal property; three years: for assault, battery, slander and libel.

Virginia: fifteen years: for mortgages, deeds of trust and liens reserved for unpaid purchase money; ten years: for recovery of lands west of Allegheny Mountains; for contracts or awards under seal unless otherwise provided for; five years: on written contracts, unsealed unless otherwise prescribed; for promissory note if unsealed or if the seal is not referred to in the body of the note; for injury to real or personal property; to recover possession of personal property; three years: for oral contracts not otherwise provided for.

Washington: ten years: for the recovery of real property; six years: for a contract in writing (sealed or unsealed); three years: for waste or trespass on real property; for taking, detaining or injuring personal property or for the recovery thereof; for contract or liability not in writing; two years: for libel, slander, assault and battery.

West Virginia: ten years: for recovery of real property; for recovery of money upon an indemnifying bond taken under any statute or upon a bond; on any note or other contract in writing, sealed or unsealed, signed by the party or agent; five years: for contracts other than those already mentioned; one year: for personal actions for which no other limitation is prescribed.

Wisconsin: sixty years: to enforce easement or covenant restricting use of real estate in recorded instrument; twenty years: on sealed instrument when cause of action accrued within the state; ten years: on sealed instrument when cause of action accrued outside the state; for actions for which no other limitation is provided; six years: on contract or for payment of money on contract, obligation or liability, express or implied; for trespass on real property; for taking, detaining or injuring goods or chattels; for specific recovery of personal property; for any injury to person or rights of another not arising on contract; two years: for death, libel, assault and battery.

Wyoming: ten years: for recovery of real property; for contract or promise in writing; for any action for which there is no other limitation fixed; eight years: for contract not in writing; four years: for trespass on real property; for taking, detaining or injuring personal property including actions for specific recovery of personal property; one year: for libel, slander, assault and battery.

C. *Effects of Prescription as an Exception*

When the exception of prescription is determined to be valid as a result of the application of the laws just indicated it will be effective in eliding the action of the plaintiff.

The exception will be found to be valid for one of two reasons, depending upon the nature of the cause in question, viz., first, because the acquisitive prescription (adverse possession or prescription in American Civil Law) has given the one who holds the property the proper title to it inasmuch as the conditions required by law have been fulfilled. Any action that seeks to compel the holder to return the property will be quashed by virtue of the exception of prescription. Secondly, an action of the plaintiff may be set aside because the liberative prescription (limitation of actions in American Civil Law) denies a plaintiff the right to pursue his action because the law has specified a limited period for placing the particular action.

Since prescription is a simple peremptory exception it should be placed after the joinder of issue and settled as an incidental question.[98]

The parties concerned in the cause must place the exception unless the issue is of a public nature, in which case the judge must advert to it *ex officio*.[99] In a purely private matter, if the defendant fails to raise the exception of prescription, the judge will allow the case to proceed without adverting to the exception, presuming that the defendant waives his right to place the exception. However, the defendant may raise the exception in the instance of appeal.[100]

It seems that an interlocutory sentence should be required to settle this exception, since extensive proofs and a number of witnesses may be required to establish the facts. However, if the matter is of little importance, or if the parties so agree, a mere decree will suffice.[101]

[98] Canon 1629, § 2.

[99] Canon 1618; Roberti, *De Processibus*, n. 226.

[100] Cf. Connolly, *Appeals*, pp. 69, 70.

[101] Wernz-Vidal, *Ius Canonicum*, VI, n. 548; Coronata, *Institutiones*, n. 1372.

CHAPTER VII

DILATORY EXCEPTIONS

DILATORY exceptions have the effect of delaying the trial. The suit will proceed as soon as the defect which retards the action is rectified.

A mere decree should suffice to settle all dilatory exceptions, because an extensive investigation should not be necessary to establish the facts upon which such an exception would be based.[1]

ARTICLE 1. INCOMPETENCY

Incompetency is a lack of jurisdiction in a judge in relation to the cause or controversy submitted to him. Hence an incompetent judge is one who is prohibited by law from considering and deciding certain causes submitted to his jurisdiction.[2] The incompetency involved may be either absolute or relative. Absolute incompetency is had when a cause is entirely taken away from the jurisdiction of a judge, either by reason of the nature of the cause itself, or because of the person to be judged, or, finally, because of the particular stage of the judgment. Such incompetency is present in an inferior judge in relation to causes reserved or legitimately called to a higher tribunal or brought to a higher instance by means of an appeal. This is also the case in relation to those persons who, by regulation of law, are subject only to the tribunal of a higher judge.

Relative incompetency, on the other hand, is had in relation to persons, causes and instances, which are not of their nature taken out of the jurisdiction of a particular judge, but in which *de facto* there is no legitimate title recognized by law in virtue of which a particular person in such a cause or in a certain stage of the trial may actually be subject to the jurisdiction of this particular judge.

[1] Wernz-Vidal, *Ius Canonicum,* VI, n. 548; Coronata, *Institutiones,* n. 1372.

[2] Cf. Bouix, *De Iudiciis Ecclesiasticis,* I, 122; Noval, *De Iudiciis,* n. 58; Lega, *De Iudiciis Ecclesiasticis,* I, n. 318; Wernz-Vidal, *Ius Canonicum,* VI, n. 46.

In such a case, then, the particular cause or person is taken from the jurisdiction of the particular judge merely for an incidental reason.[3]

Absolute incompetence is based upon principles of public law and aims at preserving the juridical order for the public good. Thus certain causes cannot be subjected to the jurisdiction of any judge except the one indicated in the law despite the fact that the ordinary norms of deciding the proper forum [4] would permit the contrary.[5] Any judge other than the one so determined is understood to be absolutely incompetent in this particular cause.[6]

The causes in which other judges are absolutely incompetent are listed in canons 1556 and 1557. Canon 1556 states that the Holy Father can be judged by no one. In other words, no one is competent to judge the person of the Roman Pontiff. The causes reserved to the Holy See in such a manner as to render the incompetence of all other judges absolute are enumerated in canon 1557. The causes of the following persons are reserved personally to the Pope: (a) rulers of governments, their children and those who are next in the line of succession; (b) Cardinals; (c) Legates of the Holy See, and in criminal cases bishops, both residential and titular. To the Tribunals of the Holy See are reserved those causes which pertain to: (a) residential bishops in contentious matters; (b) dioceses and other ecclesiastical moral persons who do not have a superior under the Roman Pontiff, viz., exempt religious organizations, monastic congregations, etc. Other causes which the Roman Pontiff has cited to his tribunal can be judged only by the judge whom the Roman Pontiff himself shall have appointed.[7]

Canons 1560-1568 give the various titles by which an ecclesiastical judge is competent in a particular cause. If the judge has none of these titles he is relatively incompetent.[8] A fundamental norm in

[3] Cf. Wernz-Vidal, *Ius Canonicum,* VI, n. 47.

[4] Canons 1561-1568.

[5] Cf. Noval, *De Iudiciis,* n. 59; Wernz-Vidal, *Ius Canonicum,* VI, n. 47.

[6] Canon 1558.

[7] Canon 1557.

[8] Canon 1559, §§ 1, 2. Cf. Noval, *De Iudiciis,* n. 69; Eichmann, *Das Prozeszrecht des Codex Iuris Canonici* (Paderborn: Schöningh, 1921), n. 48

this matter is that the plaintiff must accept the forum of the defendant. If, however, the defendant has various courts that are competent in the cause, the plaintiff has the right to choose between the courts.[9]

The law assigns a necessary forum for certain causes. These are enumerated in canon 1560, which specifies the tribunals in which these causes must be decided, viz.: (1) Actions concerning the recovery of property are to be tried before the ordinary where the property is located.[10] (2) Causes regarding a benefice (even though non-residential) are to be tried before the ordinary of the place where the benefice is located.[11] If the cause involves benefices in two different dioceses, the tribunal of either ordinary may be chosen.[12] (3) Causes which concern the administration of property must be tried before the ordinary where the administration took place.[13] (4) Causes regarding pious bequests or legacies are to be tried before the local ordinary of the domicile of the testator, except when there is question merely of the execution of a legacy, which is to be settled according to the ordinary rules of competency.[14]

As regards other causes, the following titles determine the competent forum in the first instance: domicile or quasi-domicile; the location of the thing in controversy; the place of the contract; the place of the crime; and the interrelation of causes.[15] The domicile is the principal means of determining a competent forum. Domicile is established by the taking up of residence in a place with the intention of remaining there perpetually, or by the actual residence in the place for the space of ten years.[16] A quasi-domicile also determines a competent forum. This is had by the actual residence in a place with intention of remaining there for the greater part of

(hereafter cited *Das Prozeszrecht*); Vermeersch-Creusen, *Epitome*, III, n. 16; Roberti, *De Processibus*, I, n. 56; Wernz-Vidal, *Ius Canonicum*, VI, nn. 62-63.

[9] Canon 1559, § 3.

[10] Canon 1560, 1°.

[11] Canon 1560, 2°.

[12] Wernz-Vidal, *Ius Canonicum*, VI, n. 53; Roberti, *De Processibus*, n. 60.

[13] Canon 1560, 3°.

[14] Canon 1560, 4°; cf. canons 1561-1568.

[15] Cf. Wernz-Vidal, *Ius Canonicum*, VI, n. 52.

[16] Canons 1561, § 1; 92, § 1.

the year, or even without this intention if the residence has actually extended over the greater part of a year.[17] Any person, then, who is not otherwise exempt, may be cited before the ordinary of his domicile or quasi-domicile, who exercises jurisdiction over him even though he be absent.[18]

A stranger in Rome may be cited before the Roman tribunal [19] but he has the right of having the case remitted to his own ordinary.[20] In neither the right of having the case remitted to one's own ordinary, nor in that of being cited before the Roman tribunals is there an application of the *exceptio declinatoria fori,* for in these cases there is no question of incompetency, but rather a privilege allowing a choice of tribunals.[21] A *vagus,* that is, a person who has nowhere either a domicile or a quasi-domicile, has his proper forum in the place where he is actually residing. And a religious has his proper forum in the place where the religious house to which he belongs is located.[22]

Another title determining the competent forum is that of the location of the thing, about which there is a controversy. When the suit is brought directly against the thing itself, that is in real, not personal actions, a defendant may be cited in the place where the property is located.[23]

[17] Canons 1561, § 1; 92, § 2.

[18] Canon 1561, § 2.

[19] The competent tribunal in question is that of the Vicariate of Rome, not that of the Holy See. This seems evident because the Sacred Rota is not a tribunal of the first instance except for those causes which are reserved to the tribunals of the Apostolic See in canon 1557, § 2, and other cases which the Roman Pontiff cites to his court and commits to the Sacred Rota (canon 1559, § 2). This opinion is defended by Noval, *De Iudiciis,* n. 77; Roberti, *De Processibus,* I, n. 67; Coronata, *Institutiones,* n. 1103; Beste, *Introductio in Codicem,* p. 762. Wernz-Vidal, however, hold to the opinion that the Sacred Rota is the competent court in this case.—*Ius Canonicum,* VI, n. 55, note 18.

[20] Canon 1562, § 2.

[21] Coronata, *Institutiones,* n. 1103; Reiffenstuel, lib. II, tit. II, n. 108; Augustine, *Commentary,* VII, 119.

[22] Canon 1563.

[23] Canon 1564; cc. 3, 20, X, *de foro competenti,* II, 2; Wernz, *Ius Decre-*

A competent forum may also be determined by reason of a contract. Thus by reason of a contract a party may be cited before the ordinary of the place where the contract was made or where it must be executed. The place where the obligation is to be fulfilled or urged may also be determined as part of the contract itself.[24]

A defendant may be cited in the place where a crime was committed, the judge of that tribunal being competent *ratione delicti*. If the defendant should leave the place of the crime, this same judge still has the right to recall him for trial.[25]

When two judges are equally competent, the one who has first issued a legitimate citation has the right to consider the case.[26]

As mentioned above, the plaintiff has the right of choosing any of the defendant's courts which are competent in the cause. Thus the defendant could be cited in the place of his domicile, or of any of his domiciles, if he had several. The same is true of the place of any of his quasi-domiciles.[27] In regard to citing a defendant in the place of contract a response from the Pontifical Commission for the authentic interpretation of the Code shows the fact that this is not a necessary forum, and hence the defendant cannot be brought back there ordinarily if he has left.[28]

Although the judge should consider the matter of his competence before the trial gets under way, that is, before the citation,[29] if an exception of this kind is proposed during the trial the judge himself is to decide it.[30] The judge in question here is either the ordinary or the delegated judge. And this rule stands regardless of whether

talium, V, n. 289; Pirhing, lib. II, tit. II, n. 48; Schmalzgrueber, lib. II, tit. II, n. 51; Bouix, *De Iudiciis Ecclesiasticis*, I, 298.

[24] Canon 1565, §§ 1, 2; cc. 17, 20, X, *de foro competenti*, II, 2; Schmalzgrueber, lib. II, tit. II, nn. 32, 41, 44; Bouix *De Iudiciis Ecclesiasticis*, I, 289.

[25] Canon 1566; cc. 14, 20, X, *de foro competenti*, II, 2; Wernz, *Ius Decretalium*, V, n. 290.

[26] Canon 1568.

[27] Canon 1562. Cf. Eichmann, *Das Prozesszrecht*, n. 45; Reiffenstuel, lib. II, tit. II, n. 42; Wernz-Vidal, *Ius Canonicum*, VI, n. 54.

[28] *Pontificia Commissio Interpretationis*, 14 iul. 1922, ad XII *AAS*, XIV (1922), 529 (hereafter referred to with the symbol P.C.I.).

[29] Canon 1609, § 1.

[30] Canon 1610, § 1.

he is alone or a member of a collegiate tribunal, because the canon makes no distinction.[31] The purpose of this regulation is to avoid useless and unnecessary delays.[32]

Jurisdiction exercised by an absolutely incompetent judge is invalid *ipso facto* and the sentence pronounced by him labors under an irremediable nullity.[33] When an exception is available against absolute incompetency, it may be proposed at any time. Moreover, an appeal may be made to a higher tribunal within ten days if the judge or the tribunal either admits or rejects the exception of absolute incompetence.[34] This exception of absolute incompetency may never be waived by the parties concerned.[35] The judge himself is bound to indicate this exception, and he must do so in any part of the trial in which he may advert to it.[36] This is necessary because a matter of public policy is involved.[37] A cause decided by a judge laboring under absolute incompetency never becomes a *res iudicata,* and the exception of nullity of the sentence can always be placed, whereas the action of nullity can be placed only within 30 years of the day of the publication of the sentence.[38] A sentence handed down by an absolutely incompetent judge is ordinarily not appealed because it can be attacked by the remedy of plaint of nullity.[39]

The exception of relative incompetency may be placed only by the parties themselves and, as a rule, only before the joinder of issue.[40]

[31] Noval, *De Iudiciis,* n. 193.

[32] Doheny, *Canonical Procedure in Matrimonial Cases,* p. 66.

[33] Canon 1892, 1°. Cf. Noval, *De Iudiciis,* n. 59.

[34] Cf. S.C. de Sacr., instr. 15 aug. 1936, art. 29—*AAS,* XXVIII (1936), 320; Beste, *Introductio in Codicem,* p. 776; Coronata, *Institutiones,* n. 1144; Noval, *De Iudiciis,* n. 193; Vermeersch-Creusen, *Epitome,* III, n. 60.

[35] Coronata, *Institutiones,* n. 1094.

[36] Canon 1611.

[37] Canon 1619, § 2.

[38] Canon 1892. Cf. Wernz-Vidal, *Ius Canonicum,* n. 50.

[39] Canon 1880, n. 3. Cf. Coronata, *Institutiones,* n. 1144; Roberti, *De Processibus,* n. 153.

[40] Canon 1628, § 1.

It may not be placed afterwards, unless the incompetence develops after that time, or unless the defendant did not know before that it existed. This latter fact must be attested under oath.[41] If the exception is not placed before the joinder of issue and neither of the two above mentioned excuses is shown, the acts of the trial and the sentence rendered by the judge will be valid.[42] Moreover, there is no appeal from the decision of the judge who declares himself competent when only relative competency is involved.[43] For in such an instance, as in the case of the omission of an exception, the public good demands that the law itself supply the competency of the judge when it is lacking, lest otherwise an opportunity be given to litigants of bad faith to vex and annoy their opponent by necessitating useless expenses.[44]

As mentioned above, the judge is to decide in the exception of both absolute and relative incompetence. However, in both cases judges who rashly declare themselves competent are bound to any expenses caused thereby and may be punished accordingly, even to the extent of deprivation of office, by the local ordinary, or if the bishop has been guilty, by the Apostolic See. The proceedings against such a judge may be instituted either at the request of the parties or even *ex officio*.[45]

Whenever the judge declares himself to be incompetent, either absolutely or relatively, the party who feels himself injured by this decision may appeal it to a higher tribunal within ten days.[46] The reason for this is evidently that such a declaration often causes hardship and even notable expense to the parties if the cause must be brought to another tribunal, which very often is at some distance.[47]

[41] Canon 1628, § 1.

[42] Coronata, *Institutiones*, n. 1094; Eichmann, *Das Prozeszrecht*, nn. 42, 43; Noval, *De Iudiciis*, nn. 59, 60, 68, 70; Vermeersch-Creusen, *Epitome*, III, n. 10; Lega, *De Iudiciis Ecclesiasticis*, I, n. 319; Roberti, *De Processibus* n. 55.

[43] Canon 1610.

[44] Wernz-Vidal, *Ius Canonicum*, VI, n. 63.

[45] Canon 1625, § 1. Cf. Wernz-Vidal, *Ius Canonicum*, n. 62.

[46] Canon 1610, § 3.

[47] Beste, *Introductio in Codicem*, p. 776.

Article 2. Suspicion

A judge is not to consider a cause in which he himself may be personally involved by reason either of consanguinity or of affinity in any degree of the direct line and in the first and second degrees of the collateral line, by reason of guardianship, administration, friendship, enmity, business, or by reason of its being a cause in which he formerly acted as an advocate or procurator. A promoter of justice and a defender of the bond are excluded under the same circumstances.[48]

Coronata [49] and Muñiz [50] hold this enumeration to be merely demonstrative, while Roberti [51] thinks it to be all-inclusive. Doheny [52] indicates that "considered in the light of strict obligation to refrain from judging, the enumeration can be considered as taxative. If considered in the light of optional withdrawal from a case, the enumeration would appear to be not taxative, but rather demonstrative." However, it seems that the enumeration is demonstrative under any circumstances, for the purpose of the law is to exclude a personal interest in the cause, and not all possible cases of that nature are enumerated here. For example, a judge who is also the pastor of the person whose case is brought before his tribunal may not feel obliged by reason of friendship to have another judge substituted for him, but still he should feel bound to do so by reason of the parochial bond since his judgment could be prejudiced on that account. It is possible, for example, that he might be influenced by some knowledge of the cause acquired outside the courtroom by reason of his pastoral supervision.

This exception of suspicion against the judge or other members of the court is to be proposed before the joinder of issue.[53] The plaintiff proposes it in writing when he stands in judgment, and the defendant proposes it likewise in writing when, after being cited, he first

[48] Canon 1613.

[49] *Institutiones*, n. 1146.

[50] *Procedimientos Eclesiásticos*, III, n. 147.

[51] *De Processibus*, n. 156.

[52] *Canonical Procedure in Matrimonial Cases*, p. 69.

[53] Canons 1617, 1628, § 1; Coronata, *Institutiones*, n. 1146; Muñiz, *Procedimientos Eclesiásticos*, III, n. 150; Wernz-Vidal, *Ius Canonicum*, VI, n. 151.

comes into court. However, this exception may be placed later in the trial if cause is later given for suspicion, or if it is learned only later. In this latter case the one proposing the exception must affirm under oath that he did not before know of the cause for the suspicion. This is to prevent the party from unduly complicating the case and unjustly vexing his adversary.[54] As Muñiz rightly points out, those who are responsible for proposing the exception without some cause for thinking that it exists should be made to pay any damages resulting.[55]

The procedure in judging the exception of suspicion is outlined in canon 1614. The Code there indicates the one to judge of such an exception. Thus, if the exception is proposed against the single delegated judge or against the entire tribunal or the majority of the delegated judges, it is to be considered by the delegating judge; if the exception is raised against one or the other of the several delegated judges (even the presiding judge), the other delegated judges rule on it.[56] If the exception is against an Auditor of the Rota it is to be settled by the Apostolic Signatura; [57] if it is against a member of the Signatura, it is to be settled by the other members of the tribunal, according to Roberti. He also mentions that if it is against the greater part or the entire body of the Signatura, it will be settled by the Roman Pontiff.[58]

If the exception is raised against the *officialis* or the *vice-officialis*, the bishop will judge the exception; [59] if it is invoked

[54] Canon 1628; Wernz-Vidal, *Ius Canonicum*, VI, n. 151.

[55] *Op. cit.*, III, n. 145.

[56] Canon 1614, § 1. From canons 1577 and 1578 it could appear that the presiding judge would always have to be either the *officialis* or *vice-officialis*. However, canon 1614, § 1, definitely shows that another judge can be delegated in a particular cause. Noval (*De Iudiciis*, n. 126) says that what is said in canon 1577, § 2, of the *officialis* is to be understood of any other presiding judge. Evidently, then, there is an opportunity for appointing a delegate judge.

[57] Canons 1614, § 1; 1603, § 1, 2°.

[58] *De Processibus*, n. 157.

[59] Wernz-Vidal, *Ius Canonicum*, IV, n. 148; Noval, *De Iudiciis*, n. 198. Coronata (*Institutiones*, n. 1146) holds that if the *officialis* is the president of a collegiate tribunal the other members of the tribunal may decide the excep-

against an auditor, the principal judge will be the judge of the exception. If the bishop is the judge and the exception is proposed against him, he should either substitute some one else or commit the settlement of the exception to the court which is immediately superior. If the ordinary is a Metropolitan, or an Archbishop lacking suffragans, or an ordinary of a diocese immediately subject to the Holy See, the immediately higher court is not that of the Holy See, but the one chosen by them for cases of appeal according to canon 1594, § 2.[60]

If the exception is placed against the promoter of justice, the defender of the bond or other members of the court, the presiding judge in the collegiate tribunal is to settle the exception. If there is only one judge in the case he is to settle it.[61]

The exception is to be settled as soon as possible after the parties, the promoter of justice or the defender of the bond (if the cause requires their presence and they themselves are not suspect) have been heard. The law requires also that this exception be settled as expeditiously as possible.[62] An expeditious settlement implies that the exception may be proposed orally and decided extrajudicially, not requiring a great number of witnesses or entailing undue delays.[63] A judicial form need not be observed; a mere decree will suffice.[64] Then, proofs which require a long extended time should be rejected unless other proofs are not sufficient;[65] questions should be brief;[66] objections against witnesses should not

tion, but he says that the solution of the question depends upon which quality prevails, that of being *officialis* or that of being the presiding judge of the tribunal. Noval (*De Iudiciis*, n. 198), Roberti, (*De Processibus*, I, n. 157), Wernz-Vidal (*Ius Canonicum*, VI, n. 148) and Muñiz (*Procedimientos Eclesiásticos*, III, n. 149) all hold to the strict wording of the Code which states that the bishop is to decide.

[60] Noval, *De Iudiciis*, n. 197.

[61] Canon 1614, § 3.

[62] Canon 1616.

[63] Coronata, *Institutiones*, n. 1146; Noval, *De Iudiciis*, n. 201; Doheny, *Canonical Procedure in Matrimonial Cases*, p. 73. Cf. canons 1838; 1840, §§ 1, 2; 1762.

[64] Canon 1840, § 1.

[65] Canon 1749.

[66] Canon 1775.

be deferred beyond three days; [67] witnesses should not be called again concerning the same matter unless it is really necessary.[68] Unnecessary exceptions against the testimony should not be admitted.[69] And all drawing out of the defense pleas should be moderated.[70] Finally, the decision, even though the judicial form is not observed, should express briefly the reasons in fact and in law on which it is based.[71]

If it is decided that the exception is well founded, suspect personnel are to be relieved of their duties for the particular case in question. The ordinary is to appoint substitutes; the instance of the trial, however, is not changed.[72] When the ordinary himself is declared suspect by the court of appeal, the superior of this court of the next instance is to name the substitute.[73]

There was a dispute among pre-Code authors as to whether the acts placed by a suspected judge were valid. One opinion held that such acts were *ipso iure* null. Thus Zoesius, in insisting that it was necessary to justice that trials proceed without taint of suspicion, maintained that all these acts were invalid.[74] Others held with Pirhing that such acts were not invalid *ipso iure* but merely rescissible by appeal.[75] Reiffenstuel [76] and Santi [77] held that the validity depended upon the final decision. Thus, if the suspicion was proved, the acts were of no value whether they were valid or not. De Angelis [78] also followed this opinion. He pointed out that if the arbiters eventually decided that the suspicion was unfounded the acts were valid; otherwise they were invalid, namely when there was really

[67] Canon 1764.

[68] Canon 1781.

[69] Canon 1783.

[70] Canon 1864.

[71] Canon 1840, § 3.

[72] Canons 1615; 1574; 1586.

[73] Canon 1615, § 3.

[74] Lib. II, tit. XXVIII, n. 38; cf. also De Luca, *Theatrum Veritatis et Iustitiae* (16 vols., Coloniae Agrippinae, 1706), tom. VII, Disc. III, n. 71.

[75] Lib. II, tit. XXVIII, n. 277.

[76] Lib. II, tit. XXVIII, n. 326.

[77] Lib. II, tit. XXVIII, n. 52.

[78] *Praelectiones*, lib. II, tit. XXVIII, n. 328.

cause for suspicion. The Rota judges in one instance, before the Code, maintained that under the more probable view, the acts of a suspected judge were *ipso iure* null.[79]

This same question is still in dispute after the Code. Some of the authors, insisting on the fact that an essential condition for a valid process is lacking in such an instance, hold that the acts are *ipso iure* null.[80] However, the more probable opinion appears to be that which is supported by Wernz-Vidal [81] and Muñiz,[82] and which holds that the acts are valid but rescissible. This opinion is based on the fact that canon 11 points out that only those laws are invalidating in which the act is said to be null i.e., expressly or equivalently. Since there is no provision in the Code, either expressly or equivalently indicated, stating the invalidity of the judicial acts of a suspect judge, they should be considered as valid. The suspicion, however, will be the basis of a rescissory action according to which the entire cause will be reviewed by a non-suspect judge.[83]

Article 3. Excommunication

Pre-Code law distinguished major and minor excommunication. These terms "major" and "minor" indicated that the penalty inflicted was proportioned to the gravity of the delict committed.[84] Minor excommunication implied the denial of the sacraments to the one thus penalized, while the person still retained membership in the body of the faithful.[85]

[79] "Ipsa ratio dictat, suspectos et inimicos, iudices esse non posse. Certe probabilior est sententia, acta esse de se nulla."—S.R.R., *coram* R.P.D. Lega, 31 maii, 1912, decis. XXIII, n. 8—*Decisiones,* IV (1917), 279.

[80] Roberti, *De Processibus,* n. 158; Lega-Bartoccetti, *Commentarius,* I, 229.

[81] *Ius Canonicum,* VI, n. 151.

[82] *Procedimientos Eclesiásticos,* III, n. 152.

[83] Canon 1684.

[84] Schmalzgrueber, lib. V, tit. XXXIX, n. 211.

[85] C. 10, X, *de clerico excommunicato, deposito, vel interdicto ministrante,* V, 27. The *latae sententiae* penalty of minor excommunication was abrogated by the Constitution *"Apostolicae Sedis,"* issued on October 12, 1869.—*Fontes,* n. 552. The Holy Office expressly declared that this Constitution had abrogated this penalty (Dec. 5, 1883—*Fontes,* n. 1084).

Those who were under the penalty of major excommunication were not only excluded from the reception of the sacraments, but were denied any participation whatsoever in the life of the faithful.[86] After the time of Innocent III (1198-1216), whenever the term "excommunication" was used without the qualifying indication as to whether it was major or minor, it was understood to be major excommunication.[87]

A person bound by a major excommunication could be denied the rights of a plaintiff either upon an exception placed by the defendant or by the judge's *ex officio* rejection of such a plaintiff.[88] In 1418, Martin V (1417-1431) in his Constitution *"Ad evitanda"* gave a clearer definition of the status of excommunicated persons and reduced their restrictions with regard to the ecclesiastical forum. It was thereupon no longer necessary for the judge to refuse the action of an excommunicate unless the latter was notoriously excommunicated by official pronouncement, or notoriously guilty of striking a cleric.[89] An *excommunicatus toleratus*, therefore, could enter suit and was denied the right to act only after his opponent had filed the exception of excommunication.[90] However, in those actions whose nature was rather that of a defense than an action strictly so called, and in causes in which the salvation of one's soul was at stake, any excommunicated person, even a *vitandus*, was to be admitted. There-

[86] Devoti, lib. IV, tit. XVIII, n. 4.

[87] C. 59, X, *de sententia excommunicationis,* V, 39.

[88] C. 7, X, *de iudiciis,* II, 1; c. 12, X, *de exceptionibus,* II, 2; c. 8, *de sententia excommunicationis,* V, 2, in VI°. A replication based on the fact of minor excommunication placed against the defendant by the plaintiff did not take away the effect of an exception of major excommunication placed against the plaintiff by the defendant. This rule was followed for the sake of avoiding the difficulties arising from the fact that the defendant might have talked with a plaintiff bound by a major excommunication before or during the trial, thereby incurring a minor excommunication himself (C. 2, X, *de exceptionibus,* II, 25). Even after the abrogation of the *latae sententiae* minor excommunication, the law still prohibited such contact with a *vitandus* (S.C.S. Off., 2 aug. 1893—*Fontes,* n. 1166).

[89] *Fontes,* n. 45.

[90] Cf. Pirhing, lib. II, tit. XXV, n. 20; Schmalzgrueber, lib. II, tit. I, n. 33; Wernz, *Ius Decretalium,* V, nn. 820, 835; Reiffenstuel, lib. II, tit. XXV, n. 125.

fore, an excommunicate who sought to prove that his sentence was unjust, or who was concerned in a matrimonial cause, could institute the proper action.[91] An excommunicate was to be admitted as a plaintiff also in those cases wherein the public good of the local church of which he was a member was involved.[92] Moreover, an excommunicate bound by a major excommunication, but not a *vitandus*, nor as yet publicly denounced as an excommunicate, could be admitted as a plaintiff if both the judge and the other party consented.[93]

Although a *vitandus* was to be rejected from acting by the judge *ex officio* or at the instance of the defendant, the acts placed by such an excommunicate were valid in case he was not rejected. Lega gave as the reason for this the fact that such a *vitandus* had a natural capacity under the natural law to plead, and so if he was admitted without justification, he nevertheless acted validly.[94]

The present Code of Canon Law distinguishes between only *excommunicati vitandi* and *excommunicati tolerati*.[95] A *vitandus* is to be avoided by the general body of the faithful, while one who is *toleratus* need not be avoided.[96] The latter is under a rendered judgment (*sententiatus*) after a condemnatory or declaratory sentence has been passed pronouncing the excommunication. No one is a *vitandus* unless (a) excommunication has been pronounced on him by name by the Apostolic See; (b) the excommunication has been publicly announced and (c) the fact that he must be avoided is contained in the decree or sentence. All three conditions must concur.[97]

Canon 1654 determines the status of excommunicated persons in regard to their right to stand in court. Those who are *vitandi* and those who are *tolerati sententiati* may personally institute an action in court only to attack the justice or legitimacy of their penalty.

[91] Cf. Barbosa, lib. II, tit. I, n. 10; Pirhing, lib. II, tit. I, n. 38; Schmalzgrueber, lib. II, tit. I, n. 34; Wernz, *Ius Decretalium*, V, n. 168; Bouix, *De Iudiciis Ecclesiasticis*, I, 174.

[92] C. 8, X, *de exceptionibus*, II, 25; Lega, *De Iudiciis Ecclesiasticis*, I, p. 75.

[93] Bouix, *De Iudiciis Ecclesiasticis*, I, 175.

[94] *De Iudiciis Ecclesiasticis*, I, pp. 74, 75.

[95] Canon 2258, § 1.

[96] De Meester, *Compendium*, n. 1755.

[97] Canon 2258; cf. Augustine, *Commentary*, VIII, 173.

They may, however, act in court through a procurator in order to avert any other spiritual harm. In all other matters they are to be rejected.[98] Other excommunicated persons (i.e., *tolerati* upon whom neither a declaratory nor a condemnatory sentence has been passed) may be admitted.[99] These however, may be excluded if the defendant proposes the exception of excommunication.[100]

Most of the canonists include the right to be a plaintiff in matrimonial cases among the instances wherein an *excommunicatus vitandus* or *sententiatus* may act to avert some spiritual harm.[101] Therefore, in the interest of the person's salvation any excommunicated person may be admitted through a procurator to impugn the validity of his marriage. A further question concerns the right or duty of the defender of the bond to raise an exception of excommunication in such an instance, even though no action *ex officio* need be taken by the court to exclude the excommunicated person who is impugning the validity of his marriage. Since the reason for the provision which allows him to act in order to avert spiritual harm is, as Vermeersch-Creusen state, that "what is inflicted to cure the soul (excommunication) should not be turned to its ruin," [102] it follows that such action should not be excluded by an exception. As is evident, matrimonial causes, wherein men's souls are concerned, do not partake of the same

[98] Canon 1654, § 1.

[99] Canon 1654, § 2.

[100] Canon 1628, § 3; Noval, *De Iudiciis*, n. 263.

[101] Barbosa, lib. II, tit. I, n. 10; Pirhing, lib. II, tit. I, n. 38; Schmalzgrueber, lib. II, tit. I, n. 34; Wernz, *Ius Decretalium*, V, n. 168; Bargilliat, *Praelectiones*, II, n. 1437; Lega, *De Iudiciis Ecclesiasticis*, I, p. 75; Bouix, *De Iudiciis Ecclesiasticis*, I, 174; Noval, *De Iudiciis*, n. 262; Roberti, *De Processibus*, n. 205. Doheny's statement (*Canonical Procedure in Matrimonial Cases*, p. 83, note 20) that "excommunicati vitandi aut tolerati post sententiam declaratoriam vel condemnatoriam . . . are estopped from acting as plaintiffs for the very reason that an obstacle has been placed . . . to their full and complete communion with the Church in all its workings and privileges," seems much too broad in view of the doctrine of pre-Code and many post-Code writers as cited above. Doheny quotes only canons 1654 and 2257-2267 in support of his statement. But these canons certainly lend themselves to the interpretation given above. Cf. also Doheny, *op. cit.*, p. 345.

[102] *Epitome*, III, n. 79.

limitations as private contentious causes in the matter of exceptions. The defender of the bond, of course, can and should stress the excommunication in his objection to the character and credibility of the plaintiff.

A fortiori, it can be argued that the exception of excommunication would not hold against a *toleratus* who was not sentenced, when such a one is acting to avert spiritual harm. This is the only logical conclusion of the foregoing, even though canon 1628, § 3, could, at first consideration, seem to indicate otherwise.

The exception of excommunication can be raised against a plaintiff at any period or stage of the trial, provided that it be raised before the final sentence.[103] Since the canon uses the term "gradus" which is technical in the Code for a judicial instance (stage), this exception can be raised also in the appellate instance.[104]

The exception of excommunication may be raised against the judge at any time of the trial, for according to canon 2264 an excommunicated judge cannot licitly conduct a trial. If the judge is an *excommunicatus vitandus* or has been excommunicated by declaratory or condemnatory sentence, the judicial acts performed by him are invalid.[105]

Article 4. The Procurator

An exception against a false procurator is granted to either of the parties in case the judge fails to perform his duty in rejecting a procurator who has not the proper authorization.[106] A procurator is an agent properly designated by the principal to carry on his affairs in an expeditious manner, inasmuch as the latter is either unable or unwilling to do so.[107]

[103] Canon 1628, § 3.

[104] Cf. Król, *The Defendant in Contentious Trials*, p. 109, note 90. Król also shows that a defendant can never be condemned to bear the expenses of the trial even when he postpones the entry of this exception to harass the plaintiff (*op. cit.*, p. 110, note 93).

[105] Canon 2264.

[106] S. C. de Sacr., *Instructio Servanda a Tribunalibus dioecesanis in Pertractandis Causis de Nullitate Matrimoniorum*, 15 aug. 1936, art. 49, § 1—*AAS*, XXVIII (1936), 324. Cf. further, Bouix, *De Iudiciis Ecclesiasticis*, I, 214.

[107] Schmalzgrueber, lib. I, tit. XXXVIII, n. 1.

A specific mandate to represent the principal in court is essential. A general mandate designating an individual as administrator would not be sufficient for this purpose.[108] However, the authority to represent the principal need not be limited to a single case, since it can be otherwise indicated. It may include any number of cases.[109] In the mandate the indication of the power of attorney given to the procurator must be clear; it must be given in writing with the principal's signature; the time and place of execution must be definitely determined.[110] It is necessary for the validity of the mandate that it be in writing.[111] The signature of the principal granting the power of attorney is necessary on the mandate, and its absence would be the occasion of the nullity of the subsequent sentence.[112] The matrimonial Instruction "Provida" of 1936 [113] further provides that the signature be certified by the pastor or by the notary of the curia. Further, the date and place of the signature and of the execution of the mandate must be clearly specified and are necessary for its validity.[114]

In regard to the manner of presenting the mandate an option is granted. Thus, it may be included as part of the libellus or it may be presented as a separate document.[115] But it must be inserted in the acts.[116]

[108] Canon 1659. Cf. Roberti, *De Processibus,* I, n. 210; Coronata, *Institutiones,* III, n. 1185; Noval, *De Iudiciis,* n. 280.

[109] Cf. Hogan, *Judicial Advocates and Procurators,* The Catholic University of America Canon Law Studies, n. 133 (Washington, D. C.: The Catholic University of America Press, 1941), p. 103; Roberti, *De Processibus,* n. 210.

[110] Hogan, *Judicial Advocates and Procurators,* pp. 103-107; Bouix, *De Iudiciis Ecclesiasticis,* I, 215.

[111] Roberti, *De Processibus,* n. 210; Noval, *De Iudiciis,* n. 280; Hogan, *Judicial Advocates and Procurators,* p. 104. Cf. canons 1892, 3°; 1680, § 1.

[112] Canon 1892, 3°. Cf. Hogan, *Judicial Advocates and Procurators,* pp. 105, 106.

[113] Article 49, § 1—*AAS,* XXVIII (1936), 324.

[114] Canon 1892, 3°. Cf. Hogan, *Judicial Advocates and Procurators,* p. 107.

[115] Canon 1659, § 1; Roberti, *De Processibus,* n. 210.

[116] Canon 1660.

Canon 1892, 3°, states that if the process is concluded with a procurator who is not properly authorized, and the sentence is pronounced, the sentence is irremediably null. It follows, therefore, that the exception may be placed in any stage of the trial. In order to avoid a useless procedure, this exception should be placed as soon as possible. For the same reason the judge is held to advert to this exception *ex officio* as soon as he has knowledge of the invalidity of the mandate of the procurator. Malicious delays in the matter of placing the exception may be penalized by the requiring of the payment of the expenses caused the other party as a result of the delays.[117]

Article 5. Spoliation

Spoliation consists in the act of unlawfully depriving a person of the possession or quasi-possession of an object or a right.[118] A defendent who has been the victim of spoliation may claim the *exceptio spolii* with the effect that he is not bound to answer in the case until the object in question has been restored to his possession.[119] It is to be noted that this exception of spoliation has an entirely different effect from actions concerning the recovery of property. The purpose and the effect of the action is to recover possession of the thing with its fruits, or the exercise of the right in question.[120] But the effect of the exception of spoliation, if proved, is to repel the action of the opponent for a time, that is, until he makes restitution. Thus the purpose is not precisely to obtain restitution or recovery, which in fact will not be obtained by the exception if the plaintiff prefers to desist from the action.[121] In order

[117] Canon 1629, § 1.

[118] Wernz, *Ius Decretalium,* V, n. 502; Roberti, *De Processibus,* I, n. 269; Muñiz, *Procedimientos Eclesiásticos,* III, n. 76; Coronata, *Institutiones,* n. 1228.

[119] Canons 1698, §§ 1, 2; 1699, § 1.

[120] Canon 1699, § 2. Reiffenstuel (lib. II, tit. XIII, nn. 104-155) pointed out that this restitution implied not only the restoration of the possession of the object or of the exercise of a right, but also any revenues that had accrued since the spoliation had taken place and the reparation which was due for any damages which had been incurred. Cf. also Noval, *De Iudiciis,* n. 365.

[121] C. 2, X, *de ordine cognitionum,* II, 10; Noval, *De Iudiciis,* n. 365.

that the exception may be successful the defendant must prove the fact that the object was stolen from him.[122] Two facts must be shown, viz., that the object had been possessed by the one placing the exception and that this person was deprived of the possession of the object.[123] If proof is established, restitution must be made before the trial can proceed on its own merits. Evidently, then, this exception is only dilatory, for it merely delays the trial until the restitution is made.

At times, however, the restitution of possession or quasi-possession could endanger the object or the right itself which is in dispute. In such a situation the judge, at the instance of the party concerned, or of the promoter of justice (if it concerns the public good) can suspend the restitution or give the object over to the care of a depositary in escrow who will keep it until the final sentence is pronounced.[124] Thus, if harshness or cruelty is feared, the judge can suspend the exercise of the marriage right. Or, if he fears the destruction or deterioration of the object in dispute, he can give it to a depositary in escrow.[125]

This exception of spoliation is granted not only to one who possessed the right or the object, but also to anyone who held or retained the object as a mere custodian.[126]

The exception may be used not only by a possessor in good faith, but also by one in bad faith, even if the one who effected the spoliation is the owner of the object.[127] Just as the action concerning the recovery of property, so also the exception of spoliation can be placed against anyone who effected the spoliation, or against the detainer of the thing, even though this latter is in good faith.[128] The

[122] Canon 1699, § 2.

[123] Coronata, *Institutiones,* n. 1229.

[124] Canon 1699, § 3.

[125] Cf. Roberti, *De Processibus,* n. 269.

[126] Canon 1699. Cf. Król, *The Defendant in Contentious Trials,* p. 116; Wernz-Vidal, *Ius Canonicum,* VI, n. 345. Coronata (*Institutiones,* n. 1228) denies this evident conclusion from the canon, and indicates that in such a case the exception is available only to the one in whose name the object is held.

[127] C. 5, X, *de restitutione spoliatorum,* II, 13; Noval, *De Iudiciis,* n. 365; Coronata, *Institutiones,* n. 1228.

[128] Canon 1698. Cf. Noval, *De Iudiciis,* n. 365.

fact of true ownership, together with the right of possession, or in a given case, only the right of possession, will be determined in the course of the trial. In the meantime, no one is to be deprived of the advantage of possession,[129] because if the eventual proofs should be equal on both sides a favorable decision may be effected for the possessor.[130]

Unlike the *actio spolii* which cannot be placed after a year has elapsed, the exception is perpetual and is not limited by any restriction of time.[131]

ARTICLE 6. The RIGHT TO STAND IN JUDGMENT

A defendant may register an exception against a plaintiff if the latter lacks the juridic capacity to stand in court. This exception may be based on the fact that the plaintiff has no right to sue for one of the following reasons: that he is a religious who has not the needed consent of his superior,[132] that he is a minor or one who lacks the use of reason,[133] that he is a prodigal or one who is weak-minded,[134] or finally that he is not legitimately authorized to represent the moral person concerned.[135]

A. *Religious*

According to canon 1652, religious without the consent of their superiors have no personal standing in court and hence cannot enter suit except in the following cases: (1) when they seek to vindicate against the religious organization rights which they have acquired by profession; [136] (2) when they legitimately live outside the reli-

[129] Canon 1698.

[130] Reg. 56, R.J. in VI°: "Melior est conditio possidentis."

[131] Canon 1698, § 2.

[132] Canon 1652.

[133] Canon 1648.

[134] Canon 1650.

[135] Canons 1649, 1653.

[136] Among these rights are the following: the right to remain in religion; the right to return to religion if they are expelled unjustly; rights acquired as the result of an election. Cf. Coronata, *Institutiones*, n. 1177; Reiffenstuel, lib. II, tit. I, n. 170; Lega, *De Iudiciis Ecclesiasticis*, I, n. 64; Roberti, *De Processibus*, n. 204.

gious house and the safeguarding of their rights is urgent; [137] (3) when they wish to denounce their superior. This canon evidently refers only to individual religious and not to the convent, province or order as such. Moreover, the law concerns them as religious, not as rectors or administrators of moral persons. The religious in such a position is acting not as a religious in his own name, but in the name of the moral person.[138]

B. *Minors and Persons Lacking the Use of Reason*

In causes in which the rights of minors [139] and of those who lack the use of reason [140] are involved, the parents, guardians or curators of these persons must act for them in court.[141] If the judge considers the rights of these to be in conflict with the rights of the parents, guardians or curators, or if the latter are so far distant from their charges that they cannot act conveniently, the judge should appoint a guardian or a curator.[142] In spiritual causes and in causes connected with spiritual matters, minors may act without the consent of their parents provided that they have attained the use of reason; and, if they have completed their fourteenth year, they may in these matters act of themselves; [143] otherwise they are

[137] Legitimate reasons for absence would be, for example, educational or business purposes. Cf. Roberti, *De Processibus,* n. 204.

[138] Cf. Noval, *De Iudiciis,* n. 257.

[139] According to canon 88, § 1, a minor is a person who has not completed his twenty-first year.

[140] Among these are the insane and infants. Cf. canons 88, 89.

[141] A guardian is given to a person who is incapable of acting legally because of age; a curator is given to one incapable of acting legally because of some personal defect, although he may be qualified from the standpoint of age, v. g., the insane, prodigals, etc.—Cf. Coronata, *Institutiones,* n. 1174; Wernz, *Ius Canonicum,* VI, nn. 245-252. The deaf, the dumb and the blind should be represented by a curator, unless they are sufficiently instructed and are considered capable of acting of themselves.—Cf. Wernz, *Ius Decretalium,* V, n. 159; Lega, *De Iudiciis Ecclesiasticis,* I, n. 63; Roberti, *De Processibus,* I, n. 199; Wernz-Vidal, *Ius Canonicum,* VI, n. 208; Muñiz, *Procedimientos Eclesiásticos,* III, n. 42.

[142] Canon 1648, § 2.

[143] These must, however, designate a procurator approved or to be approved by the ordinary.—Cf. Coronata, *Institutiones,* n. 1174.

to have a guardian given by the ordinary, or they may have a procurator appointed by themselves and approved by the ordinary.[144]

C. *Prodigals and Weak-Minded Persons*

Prodigals and weak-minded persons can introduce a suit in court only through their curators.[145] Curators who have been designated by the civil authority must have the approval of the ordinary before they may be admitted by the ecclesiastical judge. It may be prudent to substitute another curator for the ecclesiastical forum; such action will be decided by the ordinary.[146]

D. *Moral Persons*

The rector or administrator of moral persons whether collegiate or non-collegiate is to represent them in presenting a suit in court; in case there is a conflict with the rights of the rector or administrator in the trial, the ordinary will designate a procurator to represent the moral person.[147]

Local ordinaries can plead in court in the name of the cathedral church or of the episcopal mensal funds; [148] but to act licitly, they must consult the cathedral chapter (or the diocesan consultors) or the board of administration, securing their advice or their consent according to the amount of money involved in the case, as prescribed by canon 1532, §§ 2, 3.[149] The consent of the cathedral chapter or

[144] Canon 1648, § 3.

[145] Canon 1650.

[146] Canon 1651; Muñiz, *Procedimientos Eclesiásticos,* III, n. 44; Wernz-Vidal, *Ius Canonicum,* VI, n. 209.

[147] Canon 1649.

[148] The *mensa episcopalis* comprises whatever is necessary for the temporal sustenance of the ordinary and the members of the diocesan curia.—Coronata, *Institutiones,* n. 1175; Noval, *De Iudiciis,* n. 258.

[149] Canon 1653, § 1. Canon 1532, § 2, indicates that the counsel of the board of administration and the consent of the interested parties is required if the value does not exceed one thousand francs (approximately $200 in normal times); paragraph 3 of this same canon states that the consent of the cathedral chapter, the board of administration and of the interested parties is required if the amount is between one thousand and thirty thousand francs (normally $6,000).

of the board of administration suffices also even if a sum over thirty thousand francs is endangered. This is the case because the consent of the Holy See or of those who are interested is never required in order to stand in court, as it is for alienation.[150] In all these instances the lack of the necessary counsel or consent would not invalidate the process, since these requirements are only for the sake of safeguarding the licitness of the procedure.[151] He is, however, held for whatever damages result to the person represented.

All beneficiaries can act in the name of the benefice, but in order to act licitly they must obtain the written permission of the local ordinary, or, in an urgent case, of the rural dean, who in turn must inform the ordinary of his action.[152]

Prelates and superiors of chapters, sodalities or any other collegiate personages cannot stand in court in the name of their community without the consent of the collegiate body; the rules of the collegiate body also must be observed.[153] Religious superiors can represent their communities in a court trial only according to the specifications of their respective constitutions.[154] If the constitutions are silent on this matter, they may act both validly and licitly.[155]

In the case of negligence or of any other defect on the part of the administrator or rector of a moral person, the local ordinary or some one delegated by him can represent the moral persons under his jurisdiction.[156]

E. *Non-Catholics*

The Sacred Congregation of the Holy Office declared on January 27, 1928, that a non-Catholic, whether baptized or unbaptized, can not be a plaintiff in a matrimonial cause without the permission

[150] Cf. Roberti, *De Processibus,* n. 202.

[151] Cf. Coronata, *Institutiones,* n. 1175.

[152] Canons 1653, § 2; 1526.

[153] Canon 1653, § 3.

[154] Canon 1653, § 6.

[155] Cf. Coronata, *Institutiones,* n. 1175.

[156] Canon 1653, § 5.

of that Congregation.[157] If the judge should admit a non-Catholic without the proper authorization of the Holy Office it would be the duty of the defender of the bond to place an exception against the procedural capacity of such a plaintiff.

While the questions submitted to the Holy Office mention only matrimonial causes, and the answers given also refer only to such causes, it nevertheless seems that the same applies to all causes in which a non-Catholic acts as plaintiff. The Holy Office indicates canon 87 as the norm whereby a non-Catholic is to be excluded.[158]

In all the instances wherein the plaintiff lacks the juridical capacity to stand in court, the defendant may register a dilatory exception. This exception, if proved, impedes or suspends the case until either the necessary permission to plead is obtained, or the legitimate representative of the legally incapacitated person enters the suit. Thus, the religious must first obtain the consent of his superior, those representing moral persons must first obtain the required consent or counsel,[159] and non-Catholics must secure the consent of the Holy Office before the case can be resumed.

[157] The following questions were answered by the Holy Office: "I. Utrum in causis matrimonialibus acatholicus, sive baptizatus sive non baptizatus, actoris partis agere possit? II. Utrum in quibuslibet causis matrimonialibus inter partem catholicam et partem acatholicam, sive baptizatam sive non baptizatam, quocumque modo ad Sanctam Sedem delatis, Suprema Sacra Congregatio Sancti Officii exclusivam habeat competentiam." The replies were: "Ad I. Negative, seu standum Codici I.C. praesertim can. 87. Siquidem autem speciales occurrant rationes ad admittendas acatholicos ut actores in huiusmodi causis, recurrendum ad Supremam Sacram Congregationem Sancti Officii in singulis casibus. Ad II. Affirmative, habita ratione can. 247, § 3, et salvo praescripto can. 1557, § 1, n. 1."—S.C.S. Off., 27 ian, 1928—*AAS*, XX (1928), 75.

[158] "Baptismate homo constituitur in Ecclesia Christi persona cum omnibus christianorum iuribus et officiis, nisi, ad iura quod attinet, obstet obex, ecclesiasticae communionis vinculum impediens, vel lata ab Ecclesia censura."

[159] In regard to ordinaries acting in the name of the cathedral church or of the *mensa episcopalis*, it should be noted that they never lack the juridic capacity to stand in court in these cases, even if the necessary consent or counsel is not obtained (canon 1653, § 1). Hence the exception of lack of juridic capacity can never be invoked against them when they act in these cases. However, a dilatory exception could be placed against them because of the illicitness of their action in thus neglecting the requisites of the Code.

Since a sentence which is given in a cause in which one or the other party is not qualified to stand in judgment is irremediably null,[160] the exception against an unqualified plaintiff may be placed at any time during the trial for the avoidance of a useless procedure.[161]

[160] Canon 1892, 2°.

[161] Canon 1893.

CONCLUSIONS

1. An exception is always available as long as the facts upon which the exception is based exist and as long as the legal requirements for its presentation in court are observed.

2. Although some may be employed in the instance of appeal, exceptions as such are not available after the definitive sentence. The extraordinary remedies provided by the law which are the same as the respective exceptions in their effect must be used.

3. Ordinarily an exception of the *litis finitae* category should be settled by a judicial decree, unless extensive proofs are required to identify the exception with the cause in question.

4. *Litis finitae* exceptions are valid only if the facts of the exception and the issue involved in the new suit are identical and when the cause of pleading and the same condition of persons concur in both instances.

5. All exceptions of the *litis finitae* category have the effect of a *res iudicata* and hence enjoy the privilege of a *presumptio iuris et de iure*.

6. When a decision is rendered in favor of the admission of a *litis finitae* exception, this decision may not be appealed, but must be attacked by the extraordinary legal remedies.

7. The judge should advert *ex officio* to the exceptions *res iudicata*, compromise, arbitration, decisory oath, nullity of sentence, absolute incompetency and those placed against an incomplete tribunal, an unqualified procurator or a person lacking juridic capacity. This should be done in order to avoid a useless procedure.

8. Moreover, the judge should advert *ex officio* to all exceptions in causes wherein the common good or the salvation of souls is concerned.

9. The plaint of nullity as an exception applies only to cases of irremediable nullity.

10. The effect of simple peremptory exceptions will be determined in the rendering of the definitive sentence, for they will be judged accordingly as they affect the cause in question.

11. Simple peremptory exceptions, insofar as they influence the definitive sentence, will constitute the basis for an appeal.

12. The fear which gives the right to propose the exception of fear must be grave, either absolutely or relatively. It must be fear from without inflicted by a free human agent and must be unjust, at least *quoad modum.* It suffices if it is indirectly inflicted.

13. Dilatory exceptions have the effect of merely delaying the trial. The suit will proceed as soon as the defect which retards the action is rectified.

14. The dilatory exceptions of absolute incompetency, and those placed against a false procurator and the juridical capacity of a person to stand in court may be placed at any time.

15. The exception of excommunication may be placed in the instance of appeal as well as in a lower instance.

16. The exception of excommunication may not be raised against a plaintiff in a marriage case.

17. Acts placed by suspect personnel are valid but may give way to rescissory action.

BIBLIOGRAPHY

Sources

Acta Apostolicae Sedis, Commentarium Officiale, Romae, 1909—

Acta et Decreta Concilii Plenarii Baltimorensis Tertii, A. D., MDCCCLXXXIV, Baltimorae, 1886.

Acta Sanctae Sedis, 41 vols., Romae, 1865-1908.

Canones et Decreta Concilii Tridentini, Romae, 1845.

Codex Iuris Canonici Pii X Pontificis Maximi iussu digestus Benedicti Papae XV auctoritate promulgatus, Romae, 1917.

Codicis Iuris Canonici Fontes, cura Emi. Petri Card. Gasparri editi, 9 vols., Romae-Civitate Vaticana: Typis Polyglottis Vaticanis, 1923-1939. (Vols. VII-IX ed. *cura et studio Emi. Iustiniani Card. Serédi.*)

Codex Iuris Canonici Schemata, Lib. IV, De Processibus, I, De Iudiciis in Genere, digessit F. Roberti, Civitate Vaticana: Typis Polyglottis Vaticanis, 1940.

Corpus Iuris Canonici, 2. ed., *Lipsiensis* (Richter-Friedberg), 2 vols., Lipsiae, 1879-1881. Editio anastatice repetita, Lipsiae, 1922.

Corpus Iuris Civilis (Krueger-Mommsen-Schoell-Kroll), 3 vols., Berolini: apud Weidmannos, 1928-1929. Vol. I, ed. sterotypa quinta decima; Vol. II, ed. stereotypa decima; Vol. III, ed. stereotypa quinta.

Hinschius, Paulus, *Decretales Pseudo-Isidorianae, et Capitula Angilramni,* Lipsiae, 1863.

Jaffé, Ph., *Regesta Pontificum Romanorum,* ed. secundam correctam et auctam auspiciis Guilelmi Wattenbach curaverunt F. Kaltenbrunner (ad annum 590), P. Ewald (590-882), S. Lowenfeld (882-1198), Lipsiae, 1885-1888.

Pallottini, Salvator, *Collectio Omnium Conclusionum et Resolutionum Quae in causis propositis apud Sacram Congregationem Cardinalium S. Concilii Tridentini Interpretum Prodierunt ab eius institutione anno MDLXIV ad annum MDCCCLX, distinctis titulis alphabetico ordine per materias digesta,* 18 vols., Romae, 1868-1895.

Potthast, A., *Regesta Pontificum,* 2 vols. in 1, Berolini, 1874-1875.

S. Romanae Rotae Decisiones seu Sententiae, Romae, 1912—

Authors

[Bachofen], Charles Augustine, *A Commentary on the New Code of Canon Law,* 8 vols., Vol. VIII, *Ecclesiastical Trials,* 3. ed., 1930; Vol. VIII, *Penal Code,* 3. ed., 1931, St. Louis: Herder.

Barbosa, Augustinus, *Collectanea Doctorum tam Veterum quam Recentiorum in Jus Pontificium Universum,* 5 vols., Lugduni, 1637.

Beste, Uldaricus, *Introductio in Codicem*, Collegeville, Minn.: St. John's Abbey Press, 1938.

Blat, Albertus, *Commentarium Textus Codicis Iuris Canonici, Liber IV, De Processibus*, Romae: Collegio Angelico, 1927.

Bouix, D., *Tractatus de Iudiciis Ecclesiasticis*, 2 vols., Parisiis, 1855.

Bouscaren, T. L., *The Canon Law Digest*, Milwaukee: Bruce, Vols. I-II, 1934-1937; Supplement—1941.

Bouvier, John, *Law Dictionary and Concise Encyclopedia*, 8. ed., 3 revision by F. Rowle, 3 vols., Kansas City, Mo., 1914.

Cappello, Felix, *Summa Iuris Canonici*, 3 vols., Romae: Universitas Gregoriana, Vols. I-II, 3. ed., 1938-1939; Vol. III, 1936.

Cocchi, Guidus, *Commentarium in Codicem Iuris Canonici*, 8 vols., Taurinorum Augustae: Marietti, 1931-1940. Vol. I, 5. ed., 1938; Vol. II, 4. ed., 1937; Vol. III, 3. ed., 1932; Vol. V, 3. ed., 1932; Vol. VI, 3. ed., 1933; Vol. VII, 3. ed., 1940; Vol. VIII, 4. ed., 1938.

Connolly, Thomas, *Appeals*, Catholic University of America Canon Law Studies, n. 79, Washington, D. C.: The Catholic University of America, 1932.

Coronata, Matthaeus Conte a, *Institutiones Iuris Canonici*, 5 vols., Taurini: Marietti, Vols. I-II, 2. ed., 1939; Vols. III-IV-V, 1933-1935-1936.

Costa, Emilio, *Profilo Storico del Processo Civile Romano*, Romae, 1918.

De Angelis, Phillipus, *Praelectiones Iuris Canonici ad methodum Decretalium Gregorii IX exactae*, 9 vols., Romae, 1877-1891.

De Luca, I. B., *Theatrum Veritatis et Iustitiae*, 16 vols., Coloniae Agrippinae, 1706.

De Meester, A., *Juris Canonici et Juris Canonico-Civilis Compendium*, nova ed., 3 vols. in 4, Brugis: Desclée, DeBrouwer, 1921-1928.

Devoti, Ioannes, *Institutionum Canonicarum Libri IV*, 4. ed. Romana, Leodii, 1874.

Doheny, William, *Canonical Procedure in Matrimonial Cases*, Milwaukee: Bruce, 1938.

Durantis, Guilelmus, *Speculum Iudiciale*, 2 vols., Venetiis, 1577.

Eichmann, Eduard, *Das Prozeszrecht des Codex Iuris Canonici*, Paderborn: Schöningh, 1921.

Feeney, Thomas, *Restitutio in Integrum*, The Catholic University of America Canon Law Studies, n. 129, Washington, D. C.: The Catholic University of America Press, 1941.

Glynn, Joseph, *The Promoter of Justice*, The Catholic University of America Canon Law Studies, n. 101, Washington, D. C.: The Catholic University of America, 1936.

Gonzalez-Tellez, Emmanuel, *Commentaria Perpetua in singulos textus quinque librorum Decretalium Gregorii IX*, 5 vols., Venetiis, 1699.

Hogan, James, *Judicial Advocates and Procurators*, The Catholic University of America Canon Law Studies, n. 133, Washington, D. C.: The Catholic University of America Press, 1941.

Hostiensis, Cardinalis (Henricus de Segusio), *Commentaria in Quinque Decretalium Libros,* 5 vols. in 3, Venetiis, 1581.

———, *Summa Aurea,* Venetiis, 1570.

Ioannes Andreae Bononiensis, *In Primum Decretalium Librum Commentaria,* Venetiis, 1581.

Król, John, *The Defendant in Contentious Trials,* The Catholic University of America Canon Law Studies, n. 146, Washington, D. C.: The Catholic University of America Press, 1942.

Kuttner, Stephan, *Kanonistische Schuldlehre von Gratian bis auf die Dekretalen Gregors IX,* Studi e Testi, n. 64, Città del Vaticano: Biblioteca Apostolica Vaticana, 1935.

Laymann, Paulus, *Theologia Moralis,* 2 vols., Venetiis, 1719.

Lega, M., *Praelectiones in Textum Iuris Canonici de iudiciis ecclesiasticis, De Iudiciis Ecclesiasticis Civilibus,* 2. ed., 2 vols., Romae, 1905.

Lega, M.-Bartoccetti, V., *Commentarius in Iudicia Ecclesiastica iuxta Codicem Iuris Canonici,* 3 vols., Romae: Anonima Libraria Cattolica Italiana, 1938-1941.

Lemieux, Delisle, *The Sentence in Ecclesiastical Procedure,* The Catholic University of America Canon Law Studies, n. 87, Washington, D. C.: The Catholic University of America, 1934.

Martindale-Hubbell Law Directory, 74. annual ed., 2 vols., Summit, N. J.: Martindale-Hubbell, Inc., 1943.

Moriarty, Eugene, *Oaths in Ecclesiastical Courts,* The Catholic University of America Canon Law Studies, n. 110, Washington, D. C.: The Catholic University of America, 1937.

Muñiz, T., *Procedimientos Eclesiásticos,* 2. ed., 3 vols., Sevilla: Lib. de Sobrino de Izquierdo, 1926.

Noval, Ioseph, *Commentarium Codicis Iuris Canonici, Liber IV, De Processibus, Pars I, De Iudiciis,* Augustae Taurinorum-Romae, 1920.

Pirhing, Enricus, *Ius Canonicum Nova Methodo Explicatum,* ed. novissima, 2 vols., Dilingae, 1722.

Reiffenstuel, Anacletus, *Ius Canonicum Universum,* 5 vols. in 7, Parisiis, 1864-1882.

Ricardus Anglicus, *Die Summa de Ordine Iudiciario,* ed. Wahrmund, *Quellen zur Geschicte des römisch-kanonischen Processes in Mittelalter,* 5 vols., Innsbruck, 1905-1928.

Roberti, Franciscus, *De Processibus,* 2 vols., Romae: Apud Aedes Facultatis Iuridicae ad S. Apollinaris, 1926; Vol. I, 2. ed., 1940.

Rufinus, *Summa Decretorum,* ed. Singer, Paderborn, 1902.

Sanchez, Thomas, *De Sancto Matrimonio Disputationum Libri Decem, in Tres Tomos Distributi,* Venetiis, 1712.

Santi, F.-Leitner, M., *Praelectiones Juris Canonici,* 4. ed., 5 vols. in 2, Ratisbon, 1903-1905.

Savigny, F. K., *Sistema del Diritto Romano Attuale,* versio V. Torino, *Scialoia,* 1892.

Schmalzgrueber, Franciscus, *Ius Ecclesiasticum Universum,* 5 vols. in 12, Romae, 1843-1845.

Schulz, Fritz, *Principles of Roman Law,* Oxford: Clarendon Press, 1936.

Sebastianelli, Gulielmo, *De Iudiciis Ecclesiasticis, Pars I, De Iudiciis Civilibus,* Romae, 1906.

Sipos, Stephanus, *Enchiridion Iuris Canonici,* ed. altera, Pécs: "Haladás R. T.," 1936.

Smith, S. B., *Elements of Ecclesiastical Law,* 5. ed., 3 vols., New York, 1883-1887.

Sohm, Rudolph, *Institutionen: Geschichte und System des römischen Privatrechts,* 17. ed., Mitteis-Wenger, München: Verlag von Duncker und Humblat, 1923.

Sporer, Patritius, *Theologia Moralis, Decalogalis et Sacramentalis,* 3 vols., ed. Bierbaum, Paderbornae, 1897-1901.

Swoboda, Innocent, *Ignorance in Relation to the Imputability of Delicts,* The Catholic University of America Canon Law Studies, n. 143, Washington, D. C.: The Catholic University of America Press, 1941.

Vermeersch, A.-Creusen, J., *Epitome Iuris Canonici,* 3 vols., Mechliniae-Romae: H. Dessain, Vol. I, 6. ed., 1937; Vols. II-III, 5. ed., 1934-1936.

Wenger, Leopold, *Institutes of the Roman Law of Civil Procedure,* rev. ed., translated by O. H. Fisk, New York: Veritas Press, 1940.

Wernz, Franciscus X., *Ius Decretalium,* 2. ed., 6 vols., Romae et Prati, 1906-1913.

Wernz, F.-Vidal, P., *Ius Canonicum,* 7 toms in 8 vols., Romae: Apud Aedes Universitatis Gregorianae, Vol. VI, *De Processibus,* 1927.

Periodicals

Apollinaris, Romae, 1928—

Archiv für katholisches Kirchenrecht, Innsbruck, 1857-1861; Mainz, 1862—

Canoniste, Le, Paris, 1924-1926 (originally *Le Canoniste Contemporain,* Paris, 45 vols., 1878-1922).

Diritto Ecclesiastico, Il, Romae, 1890—

Ecclesiastical Review, The (originally *The American Ecclesiastical Review*), Philadelphia, 1889-1943; Baltimore, 1944—

Ephemerides Theologicae Lovanienses, Lovanii, 1924—

Homiletic and Pastoral Review, The, New York, 1900—

Jurist, The, Washington, 1941—

Jus Pontificium, Romae, 1921—

Monitore Ecclesiastico, Il, Romae, 1876—

Periodica de Re Canonica et Morali, Brugis, 1905; ab anno 1927: *Periodica de Re Canonica, Morali, Liturgica.*

PRINCIPAL ARTICLES

D'Angelo, S., "Un Caso di 'restitutio in integrum' nella vigente disciplina canonica," *Ephemerides Lovanienses,* III (1926), 355-360.

D'Angelo, S., "De Restitutione in Integrum iuxta canonem 1905, § 2, 4°,"—*Periodica,* XVII (1929), 37*-62*.

Hanssens, A., "De Sanctione Nullitatis in Processu Canonico,"—*Apollinaris,* XI (1938), 71-109, 215-236, 381-403; XII (1939), 198-251.

Roberti, F., "Circa limites querelae nullitatis et restitutionis in integrum,"—*Apollinaris,* I (1928), 476-483.

Roberti, F., "De Metu Indirecto quoad Negotia Iuridica praesertim Matrimonium"—*Apollinaris,* XI (1938), 557-561.

ABBREVIATIONS

AAS—*Acta Apostolicae Sedis.*
ASS—*Acta Sanctae Sedis.*
C.—Codex (Iustinianus).
Decisiones—*S. Romanae Rotae Decisiones seu Sententiae.*
D.—Digesta (Iustiniana).
ER—*Ecclesiastical Review.*
Fontes—*Codicis Iuris Canonici Fontes.*
Inst.—Institutiones (Iustinianae).
JE, JK, JL—*Regesta Pontificum Romanorum.*
Periodica—*Periodica de Re Canonica et Morali,* etc.
P.C.I.—Pontificia Commissio Interpretationis.
R.J.—Regula Juris.
S.C.C.—Sacra Congregatio Concilii.
S. C. Ep. et Reg.—Sacra Congregatio Episcoporum et Regularium
S. C. de Sacr.—Sacra Congregatio de disciplina Sacramentorum
S.R.R.—Sacra Romana Rota.

ALPHABETICAL INDEX

BIOGRAPHICAL NOTE

PAUL RAYMOND COYLE was born on December 11, 1911, at Pittsburgh, Pennsylvania. He received his primary education at St. Rosalia and St. Agnes Parochial Schools. He graduated from Duquesne University Preparatory School, Pittsburgh, Pennsylvania, in June, 1929, and received the degree of Bachelor of Arts at Duquesne University in June, 1933. Upon completing the course in theology at St. Vincent's Seminary, Latrobe, Pennsylvania, he was ordained to the priesthood on June 13, 1937. After serving as assistant pastor at St. Bernard's Church, Mount Lebanon, Pennsylvania, from July, 1937, till July, 1938, and at St. Paul's Cathedral, Pittsburgh, Pennsylvania, from July, 1938, till September, 1941, he enrolled in the School of Canon Law at the Catholic University of America in September, 1941. He received the degree of Baccalaureate in Canon Law in May, 1942, and the degree of Licentiate in Canon Law in May, 1943.

CANON LAW STUDIES *

1. Freriks, Rev. Celestine A., C.PP.S., J.C.D., Religious Congregations in Their External Relations, 121 pp., 1916.
2. Galliher, Rev. Daniel M., O.P., J.C.D., Canonical Elections, 117 pp., 1917.
3. Borkowski, Rev. Aurelius L., O.F.M., J.C.D., De Confraternitatibus Ecclesiasticis, 136 pp., 1918.
4. Castillo, Rev. Cayo, J.C.D., Disertacion Historico-Canonica sobre la Potestad del Cabildo en Sede Vacante o Impedida del Vicario Capitular, 99 pp., 1919 (1918).
5. Kubelbeck, Rev. William J., S.T.B., J.C.D., The Sacred Penitentiaria and Its Relation to Faculties of Ordinaries and Priests, 129 pp., 1918.
6. Petrovits, Rev. Joseph, J.C., S.T.D., J.C.D., The New Church Law on Matrimony, X-461 pp., 1919.
7. Hickey, Rev. John J., S.T.B., J.C.D., Irregularities and Simple Impediments in the New Code of Canon Law, 100 pp., 1920.
8. Klekotka, Rev. Peter J., S.T.B., J.C.D., Diocesan Consultors, 179 pp., 1920.
9. Wanenmacher, Rev. Francis, J.C.D., The Evidence in Ecclesiastical Procedure Affecting the Marriage Bond, 1920 (Printed 1935).
10. Golden, Rev. Henry Francis, J.C.D., Parochial Benefices in the New Code, IV-119 pp., 1921 (Printed 1925).
11. Koudelka, Rev. Charles J., J.C.D., Pastors, Their Rights and Duties According to the New Code of Canon Law, 211 pp., 1921.
12. Melo, Rev. Antonius, O.F.M., J.C.D., De Exemptione Regularium, X-188 pp., 1921.
13. Schaaf, Rev. Valentine Theodore, O.F.M., S.T.B., J.C.D., The Cloister. X-180 pp., 1921.
14. Burke, Rev. Thomas Joseph, S.T.D., J.C.D., Competence in Ecclesiastical Tribunals, IV-117 pp., 1922.
15. Leech, Rev. George Leo, J.C.D., A Comparative Study of the Constitution "Apostolicae Sedis" and the "Codex Juris Canonici," 179 pp., 1922.
16. Motry, Rev. Hubert Louis, S.T.D., J.C.D., Diocesan Faculties According to the Code of Canon Law, II-167 pp., 1922.
17. Murphy, Rev. George Lawrence, J.C.D., Delinquencies and Penalties in the Administration and the Reception of the Sacraments, IV-121 pp., 1923.
18. O'Reilly, Rev. John Anthony, S.T.B., J.C.D., Ecclesiastical Sepulture in the New Code of Canon Law, II-129 pp., 1923.

* Below n. 100 only the following numbers are still available: Nn. 3, 4, 9, 25, 34, 57 and 75. Beginning with n. 100 only the following are unavailable: Nn. 100-111 inclusive, and n. 113.

19. MICHALICKA, REV. WENCESLAS CYRILL, O.S.B., J.C.D., Judicial Procedure in Dismissal of Clerical Exempt Religious, 107 pp., 1923.
20. DARGIN, REV. EDWARD VINCENT, S.T.B., J.C.D., Reserved Cases According to the Code of Canon Law, IV-103 pp., 1924.
21. GODFREY, REV. JOHN A., S.T.B., J.C.D., The Right of Patronage According to the Code of Canon Law, 153 pp., 1924.
22. HAGEDORN, REV. FRANCIS EDWARD, J.C.D., General Legislation on Indulgences, II-154 pp., 1924.
23. KING, REV. JAMES IGNATIUS, J.C.D., The Administration of the Sacraments to Dying Non-Catholics, V-141 pp., 1924.
24. WINSLOW, REV. FRANCIS JOSEPH, O.F.M., J.C.D., Vicars and Prefects Apostolic, IV-149 pp., 1924.
25. CORREA, REV. JOSE SERVELION, S.T.L., J.C.D., La Potestad Legislativa de la Iglesia Catolica, IV-127 pp., 1925.
26. DUGAN, REV. HENRY FRANCIS, A.M., J.C.D., The Judiciary Department of the Diocesan Curia, 87 pp., 1925.
27. KELLER, REV. CHARLES FREDERICK, S.T.B., J.C.D., Mass Stipends, 167 pp., 1925.
28. PASCHANG, REV. JOHN LINUS, J.C.D., The Sacramentals According to the Code of Canon Law, 129 pp., 1925.
29. PIONTEK, REV. CYRILLUS, O.F.M., S.T.B., J.C.D., De Indulto Exclaustrationis necnon Saecularizationis, XIII-289 pp., 1925.
30. KEARNEY, REV. RICHARD JOSEPH, S.T.B., J.C.D., Sponsors at Baptism According to the Code of Canon Law, IV-127 pp., 1925.
31. BARTLETT, REV. CHESTER JOSEPH, A.M., LL.B., J.C.D., The Tenure of Parochial Property in the United States of America, V-108 pp., 1926.
32. KILKER, REV. ADRIAN JEROME, J.C.D., Extreme Unction, V-425 pp., 1926.
33. MCCORMICK, REV. ROBERT EMMETT, J.C.D., Confessors of Religious, VIII-266 pp., 1926.
34. MILLER, REV. NEWTON THOMAS, J.C.D., Founded Masses According to the Code of Canon Law, VII-93 pp., 1926.
35. ROELKER, REV. EDWARD G., S.T.D., J.C.D., Principles of Privilege According to the Code of Canon Law, XI-166 pp., 1926.
36. BAKALARCZYK, REV. RICHARDUS, M.I.C., J.U.D., De Novitiatu, VIII-208 pp., 1927.
37. PIZZUTI, REV. LAWRENCE, O.F.M., J.U.L., De Parochis Religiosis, 1927. (Not Printed.)
38. BLILEY, REV. NICHOLAS MARTIN, O.S.B., J.C.D., Altars According to the Code of Canon Law, XIX-132 pp., 1927.
39. BROWN, MR. BRENDAN FRANCIS, A.B., LL.M., J.U.D., The Canonical Juristic Personality with Special Reference to its Status in the United States of America, V-212 pp., 1927.
40. CAVANAUGH, REV. WILLIAM THOMAS, C.P., J.U.D., The Reservation of the Blessed Sacrament, VIII-101 pp., 1927.

41. Doheny, Rev. William J., C.S.C., A.B., J.U.D., Church Property: Modes of Acquisition, X-118 pp., 1927.
42. Feldhaus, Rev. Aloysius H., C.PP.S., J.C.D., Oratories, IX-141 pp., 1927.
43. Kelly, Rev. James Patrick, A.B., J.C.D., The Jurisdiction of the Simple Confessor, X-208 pp., 1927.
44. Neuberger, Rev. Nicholas J., J.C.D., Canon 6 or the Relation of the Codex Juris Canonici to the Preceding Legislation, V-95 pp., 1927.
45. O'Keefe, Rev. Gerald Michael, J.C.D., Matrimonial Dispensations, Powers of Bishops, Priests, and Confessors, VIII-232 pp., 1927.
46. Quigley, Rev. Joseph A. M., A.B., J.C.D., Condemned Societies, 139 pp., 1927.
47. Zaplotnik, Rev. Johannes Leo, J.C.D., De Vicariis Foraneis, X-142 pp., 1927.
48. Duskie, Rev. John Aloysius, A.B., J.C.D., The Canonical Status of the Orientals in the United States, VIII-196 pp., 1928.
49. Hyland, Rev. Francis Edward, J.C.D., Excommunication, Its Nature, Historical Development and Effects, VIII-181 pp., 1928.
50. Reinmann, Rev. Gerald Joseph, O.M.C., J.C.D., The Third Order Secular of Saint Francis, 201 pp., 1928.
51. Schenk, Rev. Francis J., J.C.D., The Matrimonial Impediments of Mixed Religion and Disparity of Cult, XVI-318 pp., 1929.
52. Coady, Rev. John Joseph, S.T.D., J.U.D., A.M., The Appointment of Pastors, VIII-150 pp., 1929.
53. Kay, Rev. Thomas Henry, J.C.D., Competence in Matrimonial Procedure, VIII-164 pp., 1929.
54. Turner, Rev. Sidney Joseph, C.P., J.U.D., The Vow of Poverty, XLIX-217 pp., 1929.
55. Kearney, Rev. Raymond A., A.B., S.T.D., J.C.D., The Principles of Delegation, VII-149 pp., 1929.
56. Conran, Rev. Edward James, A.B., J.C.D., The Interdict, V-163 pp., 1930.
57. O'Neill, Rev. William H., J.C.D., Papal Rescripts of Favor, VII-218 pp., 1930.
58. Bastnagel, Rev. Clement Vincent, J.U.D., The Appointment of Parochial Adjutants and Assistants, XV-257 pp., 1930.
59. Ferry, Rev. William A., A.B., J.C.D., Stole Fees, V-136 pp., 1930.
60. Costello, Rev. John Michael, A.B., J.C.D., Domicile and Quasi-Domicile, VII-201 pp., 1930.
61. Kremer, Rev. Michael Nicholas, A.B., S.T.B., J.C.D., Church Support in the United States, VI-136 pp., 1930.
62. Angulo, Rev. Luis, C.M., J.C.D., Legislation de la Iglesia sobre la intencion en la application de la Santa Misa, VII-104 pp., 1931.
63. Frey, Rev. Wolfgang Norbert, O.S.B., A.B., J.C.D., The Act of Religious Profession, VIII-174 pp., 1931.

64. ROBERTS, REV. JAMES BRENDAN, A.B., J.C.D., The Banns of Marriage, XIV-140 pp., 1931.

65. RYDER, REV. RAYMOND ALOYSIUS, A.B., J.C.D., Simony, IX-151 pp., 1931.

66. CAMPAGNA, REV. ANGELO, PH.D., J.U.D., Il Vicario Generale del Vescovo, VII-205 pp., 1931.

67. COX, REV. JOSEPH GODFREY, A.B., J.C.D., The Administration of Seminaries, VI-124 pp., 1931.

68. GREGORY, REV. DONALD J., J.U.D., The Pauline Privilege, XV-165 pp., 1931.

69. DONOHUE, REV. JOHN F., J.C.D., The Impediment of Crime, VII-110 pp., 1931.

70. DOOLEY, REV. EUGENE A., O.M.I., J.C.D., Church Law on Sacred Relics, IX-143 pp., 1931.

71. ORTH, REV. CLEMENT RAYMOND, O.M.C., J.C.D., The Approbation of Religious Institutes, 171 pp., 1931.

72. PERNICONE, REV. JOSEPH M., A.B., J.C.D., The Ecclesiastical Prohibition of Books, XII-267 pp., 1932.

73. CLINTON, REV. CONNELL, A.B., J.C.D., The Paschal Precept, IX-108 pp., 1932.

74. DONNELLY, REV. FRANCIS B., A.M., S.T.L., J.C.D., The Diocesan Synod, VIII-125 pp., 1932.

75. TORRENTE, REV. CAMILO, C.M.F., J.C.D., Las Procesiones Sagradas, V-145 pp., 1932.

76. MURPHY, REV. EDWIN J., C.PP.S., J.C.D., Suspension Ex Informata Conscientia, XI-122 pp., 1932.

77. MACKENZIE, REV. ERIC F., A.M., S.T.L., J.C.D., The Delict of Heresy in its Commission, Penalization, Absolution, VII-124 pp., 1932.

78. LYONS, REV. AVITUS E., S.T.B., J.C.D., The Collegiate Tribunal of First Instance, XI-147 pp., 1932.

79. CONNOLLY, REV. THOMAS A., J.C.D., Appeals, XI-195, pp., 1932.

80. SANGMEISTER, REV. JOSEPH V., A.B., J.C.D., Force and Fear as Precluding Matrimonial Consent, V-211 pp., 1932.

81. JAEGER, REV. LEO A., A.B., J.C.D., The Administration of Vacant and Quasi-Vacant Episcopal Sees in the United States, IX-229 pp., 1932.

82. RIMLINGER, REV. HERBERT T., J.C.D., Error Invalidating Matrimonial Consent, VII-79 pp., 1932.

83. BARRETT, REV. JOHN D. M., S.S., J.C.D., A Comparative Study of the Third Plenary Council of Baltimore and the Code, IX-221 pp., 1932.

84. CARBERRY, REV. JOHN J., PH.D., S.T.D., J.C.D., The Juridical Form of Marriage, X-177 pp., 1934.

85. DOLAN, REV. JOHN L., A.B., J.C.D., The Defensor Vinculi, XII-157 pp., 1934.

86. HANNAN, REV. JEROME D., A.M., S.T.D., LL.B., J.C.D., The Canon Law of Wills, IX-517 pp., 1934.

87. LEMIEUX, REV. DELISE A., A.M., J.C.D., The Sentence in Ecclesiastical Procedure, IX-131 pp., 1934.
88. O'ROURKE, REV. JAMES J., A.B., J.C.D., Parish Registers, VII-109 pp., 1934.
89. TIMLIN, REV. BARTHOLOMEW, O.F.M., A.M., J.C.D., Conditional Matrimonial Consent, X-381 pp., 1934.
90. WAHL, REV. FRANCIS X., A.B., J.C.D., The Matrimonial Impediments of Consanguinity and Affinity, VI-125 pp., 1934.
91. WHITE, REV. ROBERT J., A.B., LL.B., S.T.B., J.C.D., Canonical Ante-Nuptial Promises and the Civil Law, VI-152 pp., 1934.
92. HERRERA, REV. ANTONIO PARRA, O.C.D., J.C.D., Legislacion Ecclesiastica sobra el Ayuno y la Abstinencia, XI-191 pp., 1935.
93. KENNEDY, REV. EDWIN J., J.C.D., The Special Matrimonial Process in Cases of Evident Nullity, X-165 pp., 1935.
94. MANNING, REV. JOHN J., A.B., J.C.D., Presumption of Law in Matrimonial Procedure, XI-111 pp., 1935.
95. MOEDER, REV. JOHN M., J.C.D., The Proper Bishop for Ordination and Dismissorial Letters, VII-135 pp., 1935.
96. O'MARA, REV. WILLIAM A., A.B., J.C.D., Canonical Causes for Matrimonial Dispensations, IX-155 pp., 1935.
97. REILLY, REV. PETER, J.C.D., Residence of Pastors, IX-81 pp., 1935.
98. SMITH, REV. MARINER T., O.P., S.T.Lr., J.C.D., The Penal Law for Religious, VIII-169 pp., 1935.
99. WHALEN, REV. DONALD W., A.M., J.C.D., The Value of Testimonial Evidence in Matrimonial Procedure, XIII-297 pp., 1935.
100. CLEARY, REV. JOSEPH F., J.C.D., Canonical Limitations on the Alienation of Church Property, VIII-141 pp., 1936.
101. GLYNN, REV. JOHN C., J.C.D., The Promoter of Justice, XX-337 pp., 1936.
102. BRENNAN, REV. JAMES H., S.S., M.A., S.T.B., J.C.D., The Simple Convalidation of Marriage, VI-135 pp., 1937.
103. BRUNINI, REV. JOSEPH BERNARD, J.C.D., The Clerical Obligations of Canons 139 and 142, X-121 pp., 1937.
104. CONNOR, REV. MAURICE, A.B., J.C.D., The Administrative Removal of Pastors, VIII-159 pp., 1937.
105. GUILFOYLE, REV. MERLIN JOSEPH, J.C.D., Custom, XI-144 pp., 1937.
106. HUGHES, REV. JAMES AUSTIN, A.B., A.M., J.C.D., Witnesses in Criminal Trials of Clerics, IX-140 pp., 1937.
107. JANSEN, REV. RAYMOND J., A.B., S.T.L., J.C.D., Canonical Provisions for Catechetical Instruction, VII-153 pp., 1937.
108. KEALY, REV. JOHN JAMES, A.B., J.C.D., The Introductory Libellus in Church Court Procedure, XI-121 pp., 1937.
109. MCMANUS, REV. JAMES EDWARD, C.SS.R., J.C.D., The Administration of Temporal Goods in Religious Institutes, XVI-196 pp., 1937.

110. Moriarty, Rev. Eugene James, J.C.D., Oaths in Ecclesiastical Courts, X-115 pp., 1937.
111. Rainer, Rev. Eligius George, C.SS.R., J.C.D., Suspension of Clerics, XVII-249 pp., 1937.
112. Reilly, Rev. Thomas F., C.SS.R., J.C.D., Visitation of Religious, VI-195 pp., 1938.
113. Moriarty, Rev. Francis E., C.SS.R., J.C.D., The Extraordinary Absolution from Censures, XV-334 pp., 1938.
114. Connolly, Rev. Nicholas P., J.C.D., The Canonical Erection of Parishes, X-132 pp., 1938.
115. Donovan, Rev. James Joseph, J.C.D., The Pastor's Obligation in Prenuptial Investigation, XII-322 pp., 1938.
116. Harrigan, Rev. Robert J., M.A., S.T.B., J.C.D., The Radical Sanation of Invalid Marriages, VIII-208 pp., 1938.
117. Boffa, Rev. Conrad Humbert, J.C.D., Canonical Provisions for Catholic Schools, VII-211 pp., 1939.
118. Parsons, Rev. Anscar John, O.M.Cap., J.C.D., Canonical Elections, XII-236 pp., 1939.
119. Reilly, Rev. Edward Michael, A.B., J.C.D., The General Norms of Dispensation, XII-156 pp., 1939.
120. Ryan, Rev. Gerald Aloysius, A.B., J.C.D., Principles of Episcopal Jurisdiction, XII-172 pp., 1939.
121. Burton, Rev. Francis James, C.S.C., A.B., J.C.D., A Commentary on Canon 1125, X-222 pp., 1940.
122. Miaskiewicz, Rev. Francis Sigismund, J.C.D., Supplied Jurisdiction According to Canon 209, XII-340 pp., 1940.
123. Rice, Rev. Patrick William, A.B., J.C.D., Proof of Death in Prenuptial Investigation, VIII-156 pp., 1940.
124. Anglin, Rev. Thomas Francis, M.S., J.C.D., The Eucharistic Fast, VIII-183 pp., 1941.
125. Coleman, Rev. John Jerome, J.C.D., The Minister of Confirmation, VI-153 pp., 1941.
126. Downs, Rev. John Emmanuel, A.B., J.C.D., The Concept of Clerical Immunity, XI-163 pp., 1941.
127. Esswein, Rev. Anthony Albert, J.C.D., Extrajudicial Penal Powers of Ecclesiastical Superiors, X-144 pp., 1941.
128. Farrell, Rev. Benjamin Francis, M.A., S.T.L., J.C.D., The Rights and Duties of the Local Ordinary Regarding Congregations of Women Religious of Pontifical Approval, V-195 pp., 1941.
129. Feeney, Rev. Thomas John, A.B., S.T.L., J.C.D., Restitutio in Integrum, VI-169 pp., 1941.
130. Findlay, Rev. Stephen William, O.S.B., A.B., J.C.D., Canonical Norms Governing the Deposition and Degradation of Clerics, XVII-279 pp., 1941.

131. Goodwine, Rev. John, A.B., S.T.L., J.C.D., The Right of the Church to Acquire Property, VIII-119 pp., 1941.
132. Heston, Rev. Edward Louis, C.S.C., Ph.D., S.T.D., J.C.D., The Alienation of Church Property in the United States, XII-222 pp., 1941.
133. Hogan, Rev. James John, A.B., S.T.L., J.C.D., Judicial Advocates and Procurators, XIII-200 pp., 1941.
134. Kealy, Rev. Thomas M., A.B., Litt.B., J.C.D., Dowry of Women Religious, IX-152 pp., 1941.
135. Keene, Rev. Michael James, O.S.B., J.C.D., Religious Ordinaries and Canon 198, V-164 pp., 1942.
136. Kerin, Rev. Charles A., S.S., M.A., S.T.B., J.C.D., The Privation of Christian Burial, XVI-279 pp., 1941.
137. Louis, Rev. William Francis, M.A., J.C.D., Diocesan Archives, X-101 pp., 1941.
138. McDevitt, Rev. Gilbert Joseph, A.B., J.C.D., Legitimacy and Legitimation, X-247 pp., 1941.
139. McDonough, Rev. Thomas Joseph, A.B., J.C.D., Apostolic Administrators, X-217 pp., 1941.
140. Meier, Rev. Carl Anthony, A.B., J.C.D., Penal Administrative Procedure Against Negligent Pastors, XI-240 pp., 1941.
141. Schmidt, Rev. John Rogg, A.B., J.C.D., The Principles of Authentic Interpretation in Canon 17 of the Code of Canon Law, XII-331 pp., 1941.
142. Slafkosky, Rev. Andrew Leonard, A.B., J.C.D., The Canonical Episcopal Visitation of the Diocese, X-197 pp., 1941.
143. Swoboda, Rev. Innocent Robert, O.F.M., J.C.D., Ignorance in Relation to the Imputability of Delicts, IX-271 pp., 1941.
144. Dubé, Rev. Arthur Joseph, A.B., J.C.D., The General Principles for the Reckoning of Time in Canon Law, VIII-299 pp., 1941.
145. McBride, Rev. James T., A.B., J.C.D., Incardination and Excardination of Seculars, XX-585 pp., 1941.
146. Król, Rev. John T., J.C.D., The Defendant in Ecclesiastical Trials, XII-207 pp., 1942.
147. Comyns, Rev. Joseph J., C.SS.R., A.B., J.C.D., Papal and Episcopal Administration of Church Property, XIV-155 pp., 1942.
148. Barry, Rev. Garrett Francis, O.M.I., J.C.D., Violation of the Cloister, XII-260 pp., 1942.
149. Bolduc, Rev. Gatien, C.S.V., A.B., S.T.L., J.C.D., Les Études dans les Religions Cléricales, VIII-155 pp., 1942.
150. Boyle, Rev. David John, M.A., J.C.D., The Juridic Effects of Moral Certitude on Pre-Nuptial Guarantees, XII-188 pp., 1942.
151. Canavan, Rev. Walter Joseph, M.A., Litt.D., J.C.D., The Profession of Faith, XII-143 pp., 1942.
152. Desrochers, Rev. Bruno, A.B., Ph.L., S.T.B., J.C.D., Le Premier Concile Plénier de Québec et le Code de Droit Canonique, XIV-186 pp., 1942.

153. Dillon, Rev. Robert Edward, A.B., J.C.D., Common Law Marriage, X-148 pp., 1942.
154. Dodwell, Rev. Edward John, Ph.D., S.T.B., J.C.D., The Time and Place for the Celebration of Marriage, X-156 pp., 1942.
155. Donnellan, Rev. Thomas Andrew, A.B., J.C.D., The Obligation of the Missa pro Populo, VII-131 pp., 1942.
156. Eltz, Rev. Louis Anthony, A.B., J.C.D., Cooperation in Crime, XII-208 pp., 1942.
157. Gass, Rev. Sylvester Francis, M.A., J.C.D., Ecclesiastical Pensions, XI-206 pp., 1942.
158. Guiniven, Rev. John Joseph, C.SS.R., J.C.D., The Precept of Hearing Mass, XIV-188 pp., 1942.
159. Gulczynski, Rev. John Theophilus, J.C.D., The Desecration and Violation of Churches, X-126 pp., 1942.
160. Hammill, Rev. John Leo, M.A., J.C.D., The Obligations of the Traveler According to Canon 14, VIII-204 pp., 1942.
161. Haydt, Rev. John Joseph, A.B., J.C.D., Reserved Benefices, XI-148 pp., 1942.
162. Huser, Rev. Roger John, O.F.M., A.B., J.C.D., The Crime of Abortion in Canon Law, XII-187 pp., 1942.
163. Kearney, Rev. Francis Patrick, A.B., S.T.L., J.C.L., The Principles of Canon 1127.
164. Linahen, Rev. Leo James, S.T.L., J.C.D., De Absolutione Complicis in Peccato Turpi, V-114 pp., 1942.
165. McCloskey, Rev. Joseph Aloysius, A.B., J.C.D., The Subject of Ecclesiastical Law According to Canon 12, XVII-246 pp., 1942.
166. O'Neill, Rev. Francis Joseph, C.SS.R., J.C.D., The Dismissal of Religious in Temporary Vows, XIII-220 pp., 1942.
167. Prince, Rev. John Edward, A.B., S.T.B., J.C.D., The Diocesan Chancellor, X-136 pp., 1942.
168. Riesner, Rev. Albert Joseph, C.SS.R., J.C.D., Apostates and Fugitives from Religious Institutes, IX-168 pp., 1942.
169. Stenger, Rev. Joseph Bernard, J.C.D., The Mortgaging of Church Property, 186 pp., 1942.
170. Waldron, Rev. Joseph Francis, A.B., J.C.D., The Minister of Baptism, XII-197 pp., 1942.
171. Willett, Rev. Robert Albert, J.C.D., The Probative Value of Documents in Ecclesiastical Trials, X-124 pp., 1942.
172. Woeber, Rev. Edward Martin, M.A., J.C.D., The Interpellations, XII-161 pp., 1942.
173. Benko, Rev. Matthew Aloysius, O.S.B., M.A., J.C.D., The Abbot *Nullius*, XVI-148 pp., 1943.
174. Christ, Rev. Joseph James, M.A., S.T.L., J.C.D., Dispensation from Vindicative Penalties, XIV-285 pp., 1943.

175. Clancy, Rev. Patrick M. J., O.P., A.B., S.T.Lr., J.C.D., The Local Religious Superior, X-229 pp., 1943.
176. Clarke, Rev. Thomas James, J.C.D., Parish Societies, XII-147 pp., 1943.
177. Connolly, Rev. John Patrick, S.T.L., J.C.D., Synodal Examiners and Parish Priest Consultors, X-223 pp., 1943.
178. Drumm, Rev. William Martin, A.B., J.C.D., Hospital Chaplains, XII-175 pp., 1943.
179. Flanagan, Rev. Bernard Joseph, A.B., S.T.L., J.C.D., The Canonical Erection of Religious Houses, X-147 pp., 1943.
180. Kelleher, Rev. Stephen Joseph, A.B., S.T.B., J.C.D., Discussions with Non-Catholics: Canonical Legislation, X-93 pp., 1943.
181. Lewis, Rev. Gordian, C.P., J.C.D., Chapters in Religious Institutes, XII-169 pp., 1943.
182. Marx, Rev. Adolph, J.C.D., The Declaration of Nullity of Marriages Contracted Outside the Church, X-151 pp., 1943.
183. Matulenas, Rev. Raymond Anthony, O.S.B., A.B., J.C.D., Communication, a Source of Privileges, XII-225 pp., 1943.
184. O'Leary, Rev. Charles Gerard, C.SS.R., J.C.D., Religious Dismissed After Perpetual Profession, X-213 pp., 1943.
185. Power, Rev. Cornelius Michael, J.C.D., The Blessing of Cemeteries, XII-231 pp., 1943.
186. Shuhler, Rev. Ralph Vincent, O.S.A., J.C.D., Privileges of Religious to Absolve and Dispense, XII-195 pp., 1943.
187. Ziolkowski, Rev. Thaddeus Stanislaus, A.B., J.C.D., The Consecration and Blessing of Churches, XII-151 pp., 1943.
188. Heneghan, Rev. John Joseph, S.T.D., J.C.D., The Marriages of Unworthy Catholics: Canons 1065 and 1066, XVI-213 pp., 1944.
189. Carroll, Rev. Coleman Francis, M.A., S.T.L., J.C.L., Charitable Institutions.
190. Ciesluk, Rev. Joseph Edward, Ph.B., S.T.L., J.C.L., National Parishes in the United States.
191. Coburn, Rev. Vincent Paul, A.B., J.C.D., Marriages of Conscience, XII-172 pp., 1944.
192. Connors, Rev. Charles Paul, C.S.Sp., A.B., J.C.D., Extra-Judicial Procurators in the Code of Canon Law, X-94 pp., 1944.
193. Coyle, Rev. Paul Raymond, A.B., J.C.L., Judicial Exceptions.
194. Fair, Rev. Bartholomew Francis, A.B., S.T.L., J.C.L., The Impediment of Abduction.
195. Gallagher, Rev. Thomas Raphael, O.P., A.B., S.T.Lr., J.C.D., The Examination of the Qualities of the Ordinand, X-166 pp., 1944.
196. Gannon, Rev. John Mark, S.T.L., J.C.D., The Interstices Required for the Promotion to Orders, XII-100 pp., 1944.
197. Goldsmith, Rev. J. William, B.C.S., S.T.L., J.C.D., The Competence of Church and State Over Marriages—Disputed Points, X-128 pp., 1944.

198. GOODWINE, REV. JOSEPH GERARD, A.B., S.T.B., J.C.D., The Reception of Converts, XIV-326 pp., 1944.
199. KOWALSKI, REV. ROMUALD EUGENE, O.F.M., A.B., J.C.D., Sustenance of Religious Houses of Regulars, X-174 pp., 1944.
200. MCCOY, REV. ALAN EDWARD, O.F.M., J.C.D., Force and Fear in Relation to Delictual Imputability and Penal Responsibility, XII-160 pp., 1944.
201. MCDEVITT, REV. VINCENT JOHN, PH.B., S.T.L., J.C.L., Perjury.
202. MARTIN, REV. THOMAS OWEN, PH.D., S.T.D., J.C.D., Adverse Possession, Prescription and Limitation of Actions: The Canonical "Praescriptio," XX-208 pp., 1944.
203. MIKLOSOVIC, REV. PAUL JOHN, A.B., J.C.L., Attempted Marriages and Their Consequent Juridic Effects.
204. MUNDY, REV. THOMAS MAURICE, A.B., S.T.L., J.C.L., The Union of Parishes.
205. O'DEA, REV. JOHN COYLE, A.B., J.C.D., The Matrimonial Impediment of Nonage, VIII-126 pp., 1944.
206. OLALIA, REV. ALEXANDER AYSON, S.T.L., J.C.D., A Comparative Study of the Christian Constitution of States and the Constitution of the Philippine Commonwealth, XII-136 pp., 1944.
207. POISSON, REV. PIERRE-MARIE, C.S.C., A.B., PH.L., TH.L., J.C.L., Droits Patrimoniaux des Maisons et des Eglises Religieuses.
208. STADALNIKAS, REV. CASIMIR JOSEPH, M.I.C., J.C.D., Reservation of Censures, X-141 pp., 1944.
209. SULLIVAN, REV. EUGENE HENRY, S.T.L., J.C.L., Proof of the Reception of the Sacraments.
210. VAUGHAN, REV. WILLIAM EDWARD, J.C.D., Constitutions for Diocesan Courts, X-210 pp., 1944.
211. LYONS, REV. JOSEPH HENRY, J.C.L., The Joinder of Issue in Canonical Trials.

www.ingramcontent.com/pod-product-compliance
Lightning Source LLC
LaVergne TN
LVHW050214080826
844660LV00012B/408

* 9 7 8 0 8 1 3 2 2 3 8 0 3 *